Angie Barnes

Four Years in Bed . . .

and how I got up

Publisher: tredition

ISBN
Paperback   978-3-7323-9184-4
Hardcover   978-3-7323-9185-1
eBook   978-3-7323-9186-8

Table of contents

Chapter 1 – The Coming Of The Storm

For the first time in my life I felt a feeling of freedom, I was out of the rat race! Shortly after a long and unhappy marriage I met Andrew. I moved into his beautiful converted stable on the Ashdown Forest, which he had spent the last eight years restoring. He worked from home making musical instruments and it was a very relaxed lifestyle with no mortgage to pay and we went out most evenings to friends, gigs and open mic sessions.

I left my full-time, low-paid job as a gardener for a hotel and became a self-employed cleaner, choosing my hours and clients. If I didn't like a job/client, I simply left and got another one. After building up a really good reputation as a trustworthy cleaner I literally found myself with people queueing up for my services and having a long waiting list. This encouraged me to put my prices up and enabled me to be able to choose my clients. I found myself working in grand houses scattered around the forest. Most of my clients would just leave me to it. Working in these gorgeous houses I would daydream that they were my own and I was the Lady of the Manor!!

Seeing how the other half lived was very insightful. Most of the women spent many days and even weeks on their own while their husbands worked away earning huge amounts of money. These women, I realised, were often lonely and having to do all the childcare on their own. Life behind the scenes is not always as idyllic as we think it is! I even saw one of the husbands out one day with another woman but did not feel it was right to say anything so kept it to myself.

Prior to this I had done nine-to-five jobs and had to drive some distance caught up with the rush hour which really was not enjoyable. Now I was just driving round the forest, which was pretty much empty of cars. A traffic jam for me now was waiting for sheep to cross the road. My kind of traffic jam for sure! All my travel was full of beautiful sights and I truly marvelled at my new relaxed way of life. Having less travelling also meant that I had more of my own time which was great.

Watching the children in these houses I worked in, although they had many expensive toys to play with; ponies and large gardens, they never appeared any happier than all the children I had known in my own life. No children would knock on the door to play as all these houses were detached within large grounds. This meant that there were none of the street games I had played and enjoyed as a child.

These children, despite being very privileged, often struck me as very lonely and often sad. I certainly would not have swapped my childhood for theirs. Their fathers were very rarely there and I felt that they were often missing out on the important things in life.

I was very active (some would say over-active), working hard, walking the dog in the forest and swimming (usually 100 lengths a day) every day. I belonged to a local Health club and would swim and then have a steam and go in the jacuzzi. This had been a habit of mine for about 15 years at various spas near to where I had lived or worked. The full membership I had there meant that Andrew could join me sometimes as a guest.

Andrew's friend, Yvonne was asking us one day if we knew of anyone that could be her "wife". She joked that she needed a wife to pick up her children from school and look after them for a few hours each day. I told her that I thought I could do this so we agreed that we would do a trial for a week and see how I got on. She said it was obviously important that whoever she took on got on with her children and they must feel comfortable with the situation. She said she would introduce me to the children first and if they liked me I would start the following week.

The youngest child was a boy, Luke, aged 8 and there were two girls, Tess, aged 12 and Anna, aged 15. They were amazing children and we all seemed to get along and very quickly I became part of the family.

It took me a bit longer to bring Luke out of his shell but when I took him to the sweet shop and said he could have anything he wanted he suddenly brightened up and became my friend! Friday afternoons became sweet day when I would buy them all sweets which I think was one of the reasons they all liked me!

I grew to adore all 3 children and loved the job. Yvonne became a very close friend and I started to do more for her, cleaning the house and doing ironing. She was always so appreciative and paid me well.

They lived in a big rambling house on The Ashdown Forest and we spent a lot of time in the garden and the forest. Driving home on a winters' evenings as the sun set over the forest was truly magical and I would see deer on a daily basis. My life was happy and blessed.

Life was good, apart from one thing. My mum had had a massive heart attack many years before. She had a triple bypass but during that operation she had another heart attack. She ended up on a life support machine with a tracheotomy for 3 weeks. It looked like she was not going to come out of the coma and they were looking at turning the life support machine off.

Amazingly, she did come out of the coma but the recovery was, from there, very long and painful. She had lots of ongoing problems. The tracheotomy had damaged her vocal chords and so she had to have another operation. After this she found it very difficult to speak. For a long time she had no voice at all and the only way she could communicate was by writing things down. She was very frustrated. She had also now got breathing problems too. She was in hospital for a very long time and became institutionalised. When she did come home it was a very slow recovery. She never fully recovered and for many years I would go over there every day, buy food to entice her to eat, and often help her eat it. Gradually she built up her confidence, gained weight and became a lot happier. My dad had retired to look after her and between the whole family we tried to make life easier and happier for her. My sister was a great support and involved them a lot with her horses. They had bought a field for her near where they lived and threw themselves into the good life. My mum got chickens and my sister also bought some sheep. My mum and dad both loved the animals.

We all helped as much as we could to make my mum and my dad's lives easier. Sadly, at this point, my dad's health began to deteriorate as his memory slowly went and he began doing very strange things. For a long time we all tried to make excuses for him, I guess we were in denial that he had the onset of Alzheimer's.

We all attended a family funeral and at the burial my dad was just wandering around and my cousin asked what was wrong with him. I flippantly told her he was going mad and laughed. She looked very worried. At the wake another cousin said he was worried about my dad as he was acting very strangely. I did not want to hear this as I obviously did not want my dad, as I knew him, taken away from me.

One day when I arrived at my parents house my mum voiced her worries and asked if I could spend some time with dad and see what my opinion was. I suggested to my dad that I would take him to a local lake and we could go for a walk and pop into the garden centre afterwards and have some tea and cake. He was very enthusiastic at this idea as he had always been a keen walker. We pulled up at the lake and got out and went for quite a lengthy walk talking amicably as we walked. I was cheered up as all seemed well and we talked at some length on various different subjects. We then went into the garden centre and I thought I would test him on a few things. I sounded shocked and asked my dad to guess how much some conservatory furniture was convinced that if he had Alzheimer's his guess would be far out. He was within a few pounds so I felt good about this too. We sat down and had some tea and cake and all felt very well with the world.

On leaving to go back to the car he walked straight past my car and onto a narrow jetty that went out into the lake. It looked as though he was going to walk right off it into the lake and I shouted out to him to stop. He did stop but just stood there looking very confused. As hard as I tried I could not get him to turn round and come back so I slowly walked up to him, took his hand, and very slowly coaxed him back to land. When we reached the land he just wanted to go back. I was out of my depth and quite scared but eventually I got him back to the car and back home. It was hard telling mum that I too thought something was seriously wrong.

He walked into the village one day and someone found him "lost" in a skip. He kept trying to push the neighbours' cars "out of the way", chopped down a tree and then tried to build a bonfire in the middle of the living room. He had also become incontinent.

The doctor was called out and gave him a sedative so that he couldn't do any more harm that day along with a prescription for some more for him to take if he got out of hand. Luckily he always accepted anything from the doctor without questioning it.

My mum was weak and we had to accept the truth and that this could not continue as he had become a danger to himself and his family. This obviously had an impact on all of us. Our dad had always been so strong, very intelligent and nothing but a good father and husband. It was absolutely devastating to face the truth that he was now none of these things. He had also been my mum's carer so everything became very worrying.

My sister and I discussed leaving work to look after them both but dad really did need 24 hour supervision. He was also very strong and had become dangerous so, sadly, we had to admit that the best option was to find a care home for him. We both also needed some money to sustain our own lives. My mum and I looked at a few nursing homes but one of the criteria was that he was still near her. Many we approached said that they didn't want him as he was too strong and was likely to cause problems and break out. He had already broken out of the psychiatric unit of the hospital and was found wandering several miles away in his hospital pyjamas.

We eventually found what we considered a suitable place and mum and I went to talk to the matron to discuss whether it was feasible for dad to live there. She was lovely and said she thought my dad would fit in and she couldn't see him being able to escape. She asked us if we had any questions. My first question was "Could he come home if he got better?" She said yes, but nobody had ever done that before. This was quite a shock to me but I still thought my dad would be different. Mum asked if she would be able to come up whenever she wanted to and the matron said she positively encouraged visitors and there was one woman that spent all day, every day, with her husband. Mum wanted him to have a private room but the only space available at that time was a small shared room with a man called Jim. She assured us that a room would more than likely become available soon (as is the case in these situations). She told us that he would have a key-worker who would mainly look after dad. She told us we could enquire after his well-being any time and the key worker would keep us informed at all times of any changes.

We took dad in and he never asked where we were taking him and just accepted everything as it was. Sharing a room with Jim was never a problem as they never showed any recognition of each other. When I asked my dad what Jim was like, he answered, "Who is Jim?"

He did try several times to break out, the first time ramming a wheelchair into the fire escape door and another time he did succeed but only made it to the top of the drive! The staff luckily took all these things in their stride.

My life from then on became focussed on my mum and dad and I gave up a few jobs to be able to help as much as I could. I would pick my mum up twice a week and take her to see dad. We both found these times very emotional and would always be in tears every time we left. There were some special times there and some very comical ones too. But mainly it was just hugely depressing to see my dear dad unable to communicate and not even really knowing who we were.

Andrew was worried about me as I was always sad so I made a decision. I told mum that I could only cope with going there once a week and on the other day we would do something nice together instead. She was not happy with this but I was sure this was the right thing for me and suggested that if she wanted to visit more she could get a taxi or a friend to go with her.

So once a week, mum and I went shopping together or visited nice places and we saw dad once a week. I still found it difficult as my father, as I had known him, had completely gone. I would play Lego with him and try and do children's puzzles with him but his brain was not even good enough for these things. On one of the occasions mum and I were there we took dad out into the grounds and picked blackberries. He remembered how to do this and really enjoyed it. As a family when we were children we had picked bowls and bowls of blackberries each year and my mum would make pies, crumbles and jams that would last for many months. As my dad's birthday had always been around the blackberry season and blackberry pie was one of his favourite things I took the blackberries home and made him a pie for his birthday a few days later.

One day when we visited him there was a lady doing some art therapy and I was amazed at how focussed everyone was and how good their artwork was. Usually everyone just sat there in a daze looking like they were incapable of anything with blank expressions on their faces. My dad was just scribbling which was more what I expected and we just sat down quietly next to him. The art therapist came over to us and asked if my dad was a religious man and we said yes, he was and that he had been a regular church-goer and a good Christian man with a strong faith. She said she thought so as he had drawn a church. None of us had ever seen my dad draw and always assumed that because he showed no interest in art he probably could not draw. Much to our amazement she produced his drawing. It was incredibly intricate and represented perfectly the church he had attended for many years. My mum was over the moon at this drawing and took it home with her and treasured it. Sadly, for whatever reason, this lady did not return which was a great shame as for an afternoon she had brought everyone out of their mundane lives and they had all become focussed and animated and produced some amazing work.

Andrew would come with me sometimes and dad enjoyed him reading Jesus stories from a children's book. My dad had studied the Bible and obviously remembered these stories and quite clearly loved to hear them being read to him.

Andrew also played his concertina and sang the old songs like *Maybe it's because I'm a Londoner* and *Streets of London*, etc. To our utter amazement he started singing along. By this time he could not talk coherently so trying to understand him was becoming really hard. Apparently the part of the brain that we use to sing is different from the part that we use to talk and the singing part dies later. This made me realise just how important music therapy is for old people. I have since seen this happen many times and old people can find a bit of their old happy selves and have fun singing along to the old songs they remember. It is a joy to watch.

It saddens me that more therapies are not available within these care homes. I am sure if the old people could have their brains stimulated more their lives would be much happier. Instead they are left staring blankly in chairs for most of the time. I am told the budgets do not allow very much but this is hard to understand with the costs involved with putting someone in a care home. I would have been happy to pay a bit more for my dad to have had more therapies. This was something that was promised to us at the beginning but sadly never really materialised.

The strain of all of this, working and all the other normal daily tasks was getting to me. My sister and I began to bicker, she could not cope with seeing my dad (she had always been a real daddy's girl) and refused to come up. Dad had always told us that if he ended up in a home we should either put a pillow over his head or just leave him there. He did not want us visiting him and seeing him like that. I for one could not fulfil these wishes as I still loved him dearly and my mum also needed me there. We would come home with stories of our visits and my sister would get deeply upset and angered by them. She could not understand how I could play Lego with him and we would come home with funny stories like the time dad had put someone else's teeth in his mouth. She would get very angry thinking that we were laughing at him when in fact we were just trying to get through it the best we knew how. I did — and still do — use humour to get through difficult situations and I always prefer laughing to crying. I can now, of course, see both sides but I guess we were both upset and angry and taking it out on each other.

I still had quite a few cleaning jobs and I kept "pulling muscles". My neck and shoulder hurt and just wasn't getting any better. The doctor sent me to see a physiotherapist. She was bewildered and said that I had a neck of someone double my age because of how stiff it was. It felt at the time that I had no option but to soldier on.

My dad was going downhill and one day we went to see him and he was in a chair being restrained. He was angry and his eyes were bulging. He could not talk but it was obvious he wanted to get up and out. I went to find his key-worker and he explained that my dad had become violent and they had no option but to sedate and restrain him. This was very distressing for me and my mum so the key-worker got him out of the chair and said we could go to his room for the visit. On entering his room we saw that all his wallpaper was ripped and his pictures had been removed. We enquired what had been going on and were told that my dad had messed himself and rubbed faeces over himself, the bedding and the walls. I was horrified but was told this was actually quite common at this stage of my dad's illness. We stayed a while and my dad calmed down and we left.

The next time we visited the home we were told to go and see the manager. He told us that dad was showing all the signs of dying and he didn't think he had long to live.

Sure enough, a few weeks later, my beloved dad died. We were all by his bedside, including my sister, the evening before and he was quite obviously very distressed and sweating profusely. I mopped his brow and massaged lavender oil into him and he eventually relaxed and went into a deep sleep. The matron came in and told us all to go home, get some sleep and come back in the morning.

On awakening the next day I quickly got dressed and rang the home at 9am . They told me he was absolutely fine and that there was no need to rush up. Five minutes later at 9.05am they rang and told me he had died! Apparently he went very quietly and peacefully.

The matron told me she was cleaning up around her and talking to my dad as she did. My dad had amazing piercing blue eyes and she was telling him how lovely they were and it was amazing that they were still so bright and piercing. She said she turned round and he had passed away. She joked that she thought she had bored him to death. Knowing my dad as well as I did I think she may be right but I wasn't going to tell her that. She had clearly liked him and looked after him well.

Andrew and I went to get mum and the three of us went to see dad who was still lying in his bed. This was the second dead body I had seen in my life and it looked so empty as had the other one. This comforted me on both occasions as it is as if the soul has left leaving the shell of the body behind. This is what I believe happens when we die.

I kissed him goodbye and told him I loved him.

The matron enquired if we wanted to take anything of his at that time. I took my dad's hat out of his wardrobe as he and I shared a love of hats and this seemed the most appropriate thing of his to have. We then went on to have the most bizarre day I think I have ever had!

My mum was just acting like it was a normal day showing no emotion and asked if we could take her to go to the garden centre (something we regularly did together). It was one of those big garden centres that sell everything. She was just looking around everything, picking lots of things up and commenting on them. To an outsider, they would never have guessed that her husband of 50 years had just died.

We then had lunch there and Andrew, ever-practical, started talking about what needed to be done. We all agreed that it would be best to drop mum off and start doing the practical things that were needed to be done. We phoned the funeral directors in mum and dad's village and they said they would get dad and take him there. In the meantime, they told us we would need to get a death certificate.

We went to the registrar and were told we needed to get a doctor's note with a reason of death before they would be able to register his death.

We rang the doctor and he said he would issue one and we could pick it up in half an hour. We drove to the doctor's and Andrew went in and picked it up and came out to the car before actually looking at it. Getting into the car he looked at the note and burst out laughing. He said if my dad was alive he would be really chuffed as it was a sick note and he had just been signed off work for 2 weeks!

After finally getting that sorted and his death registered we headed off to the funeral directors.

They were explaining everything that would happen and said we needed to choose a coffin and they would dress dad in whatever clothes we chose for him. We said we would go and talk it through with mum and discuss it all with her before making any decisions.

We arrived at mum's and she rang my sister who went completely mad, shouting and screaming that we should not be doing all of this and that it was her job.

Andrew was obviously upset as he was only trying to help. We left them to finalise the arrangements and went home.

Soon after getting home mum rang me and said they wanted dad's hat back as they had decided he should be buried in it. I was really upset, thinking they were deliberately taking away the one thing that I wanted of my dad's. I took the hat back, gave it to them and left.

That evening Andrew and I went outside and let off a rocket to say goodbye to my dad. I found this very releasing and for the first time that day I began to feel better.

On entering the house the phone was ringing. It was my sister telling me that her dog had bitten mum's arm and she was in East Grinstead hospital in need of a skin graft!

This was possibly the craziest day of my life and the start of the collapse of my family.

I visited my mum regularly in hospital and my sister took over the arrangements of the funeral. I was quite relieved my mum was in hospital being looked after and getting lots of attention. Obviously everyone knew dad had just died and everyone was being really kind. It was sad to see my mum looking so small and vulnerable but I tried to spoil her as much as I could bringing her good food and gifts.

My dad's funeral was well-attended as he had been a churchgoer and a very popular man in the village.

Gradually, after that, things got back to some normality and I carried on seeing my mum twice a week, taking her shopping, to the garden centre and helping out with things she needed doing. My brother also came over periodically to take mum out and my sister was generally in daily contact as she lived just up the road. My sister and I became more and more distant and I actually found myself starting to dislike her. She would often be at mum's and, despite my mum having a heart condition and breathing problems, she chain-smoked around her and was always asking her for money. She would traipse in to my mum's immaculate house with muddy boots and her muddy dog in tow.

About a year after dad had died, my mum kept saying she wanted to go to Lulworth Cove again before she died. It was a place we had frequented as children and mum and dad had continued going there in their caravan long after we had all grown up.

There was a guest house really near the cove that mum had always dreamed of staying in but could never have afforded to with 3 children. I looked it up and booked us in and drove us there for a long weekend.

We did lots together, sat on the beach, took a boat trip and went to a few other local places and had a cream tea. My mum drew some of the wild flowers which she said she was going to paint when she got home. She was really relaxed and quite clearly happy to be back in an area she had loved for many decades. This was a special time for me and I felt very close to her.

By this time my shoulder was really playing me up and I was struggling to sleep through the pain. My mum was quite perplexed to see the pain I was in as I never complained and was rarely ill. I just put it down to having pulled a muscle or having strained myself in some way and not wanting to make a fuss just brushed it aside.

Little did I know then that this was the start of a condition that would completely change my life forever.

The following week I rang mum and could not get an answer. I kept ringing and ringing but to no avail. I drove to her house but it was empty. I was naturally worried but as I could not get hold of my sister, I assumed they were out together.

When I could not get hold of her the next day either I was very worried. However, on the third day, I went round there and she answered the door. On enquiring where she'd been she would not tell me but eventually told me she had gone to Somerset to look at a house with my sister.

I asked if she had any pictures of it and I was very confused as to why my sister would be moving away as she had her horses and was close to mum. I was very surprised that up to this point neither of them had mentioned that she was looking to move.

She told me she didn't have any pictures of the house. While she was making me a cup of tea I spotted a house magazine on the coffee table. On opening it, it fell open and there was a huge house highlighted there.

My sister lived in a very small house and I knew she could never have afforded anything of this size or cost so I remained confused.

When my mum came back with the tea I asked her about it. She became very flustered and very reluctantly told me that she was putting her resources in with my sister's, and would selling up and moving.

It was to be a guest-house that my sister would run and my mum was going to live in the granny annexe. I asked her when she was going to tell me and she said she wasn't going to until the day they moved. I asked if she was going to tell my brother before she moved and she said no. Horrified I told her that I thought this was unfair and I would give her a week to tell him or I would be telling him myself.

She then pointed to the driveway in the picture of the house and said that if Andrew and I wanted to come and stay, we could stay there in our campervan.

After having done so much for my mum and dad I was amazed that my mum could treat me like this. All I could think was that my sister had manipulated my mum into this. She had horses and had always wanted to live in this part of the country. It was also very obvious to me that the whole of my mum and dad's estate would be going to my sister.

I went home very upset, bewildered and very, very confused at the recent revelations. Andrew thought it must all be a misunderstanding and invited my mum over for dinner. He questioned my mum and realised that it was not a misunderstanding and everything I had told him was, in fact, true. His opinion of my mum went very downhill that evening. He had already gone off my sister way back when there was all the kerfuffle over my dad's funeral.

As usual I went round to my mum's house the following week. Andrew said to me on leaving the house to not lose my temper whatever happened or do anything I might regret.

My mum begged me not to tell my brother she was selling up and moving as she was concerned he would no longer come over and take her out.

I was absolutely appalled and realised that I had always been piggy-in-the-middle, making amends in all the family disputes. I told her I would be telling my brother and if I was honest, I was not even sure I wanted to take her out any more. Feeling totally used and abused I left her house slamming the door behind me. So much for keeping my cool!

That was to be the last time I was to see my mother.

When I have looked back on that day I have wondered whether I should have reacted differently but I still think that what she did was under-handed and cruel and I could not have carried on my relationship with her without an apology for her behaviour.

Obviously I told my brother. He was not surprised as he had always disliked my sister and saw her as a manipulative, evil and money-grabbing cow (his words). My brother and sister had never got on and I had witnessed fights between them all of my life. His hatred intensified and my hurt did too. The core of my soul hurt so much. My belief system in family had been completely crushed.

I carried on working and Yvonne was a total star. She listened to me crying and totally understood my hurt. She suggested I write my sister a letter telling her how much she had hurt me then burn it which I did.

She also did some Reiki on me. Both of these things helped me at the time. Neither my mum or my sister ever contacted me after that.

About 5 months later I bumped into my cousin who said he would like to get me, my mum, my brother and sister and bang all our heads together. He told me that my sister's house was sold and my mum's house was in the process of being sold. They would therefore be moving to Somerset very soon.

He urged me to contact my mum and make up but I said I would not be doing that without an apology from her. As I walked away I was in total shock that this was all happening.

A few weeks later I was in town looking for a birthday card when Andrew rang me on my mobile phone. He said he had received a call from my sister saying Mum had died and she hoped that I would feel guilty. She also told Andrew that we were not welcome at the funeral.

At the time I was in a hippy shop and I knew the owner. I asked her if I could sit down as I had just received some bad news. She was furious that Andrew had rung me and told me on the phone; he later said that he didn't think I would be upset as we had fallen out.

On leaving there I went to see my friend Ken who owned a cobbler's shop in the town as I was in a bit of a state of shock. He hugged me and got me a cup of tea and I stayed there until I felt less shaky and able to drive home.

My godmother, Sylvia came to see me the next day and we went for a very long walk in the Ashdown Forest and we did some screaming therapy together.

She was angry all along and I could see, within the family, everyone was taking sides. It became my gang and my sister's gang. Sylvia's son-in-law described our family as like a Mafia family!

My cousin Phil rang me, informing me that my sister was really upset and could I come over to mum's house to help with the funeral arrangements?

I do not consider myself a hard person but I was so angry, especially after the fuss she had made when Andrew and I had tried so hard to be there and help out with dad's funeral arrangements, I point-blank refused. He enquired as to whether or not we would be at the funeral and I said I was not sure.

We did go to the funeral but we sat on the other side of the church to the family. My godmother Sylvia, my brother and my friend Mandy sat with me. This was obviously noted with a lot of disapproval from other family members but I really did not, at that time, want to be associated with my sister.

The funeral was good. My sister walked my mum's coffin down the aisle with her best friend and had added a few nice touches bringing out the best parts of my mum. On the coffin she had placed a few of the amazing handicrafts that my mum had been working on. Mum was a very talented seamstress and knitter and did the most exquisite embroidery, tapestry and flower arranging.

The vicar called me and my brother to join my sister at the front of the church with the coffin and I really did appreciate that. After all, even if it had all gone pear-shaped, at the end of the day we were her 3 children and it seemed right that we were all there at the end.

We all went to the burial where my mum was placed in the double plot with my dad. At the wake Andrew suggested to my sister that she and I talked as this would probably be the last chance of any kind of reconciliation.

We both went outside to talk. She was angry, blaming me, saying that I had killed my mum (I later learned that the evening before my mum had died my sister had been shouting at her, telling her to change her will for it all to be given to her, in case she died before they moved. My mum had rung my aunt after my sister's outburst, very upset and feeling very pressured). My sister informed me that she was now going to be homeless and her horses didn't even have a paddock.

She went on to say that mum had cried over me and I asked her if she had ever thought if mum, and dad for that matter, had ever cried over her (which they had many times). She swore at me and got in her friend's car, who was waiting for her and they screeched off up the road. That would be the last time I would see my sister for nearly 13 years.

From that day onwards my health deteriorated rapidly. My feet, as well as my neck and shoulders, started hurting and it felt like I was walking on jagged rocks. It was becoming physically and emotionally more and more difficult to work.

A short while after the funeral my brother and I both received letters from my mum's solicitor asking if we would be prepared to sign our inheritance over to my sister. They stated that this was what my mum was about to do before she died and it would be the best thing for us to do to respect her wishes.

Mine and my brother's inheritance was still substantially lower than our sister's. I had a friend who was a solicitor and my brother and I went to see him.

He was outraged to hear the story and sent a very short letter stating that his clients totally accepted their mother's wish but felt that it had definitely not been their father's wish. He went on to say that because of this his clients would not sign and wished the will to stay the same.

A few days later the phone in my house kept ringing and ringing throughout the day. Andrew was out and I literally could not get down the stairs as on that day my mobility was really bad. My brother rang the next day telling me that my sister had rung him, threatening him that we would not get away with it and that we both needed to watch our steps. My brother retaliated saying, "I could have you dead in half an hour and you will be fish bait in the River Thames." He told me that he knew someone that could do this who owed him a favour and that he was going to arrange it.

I spent hours on the phone talking him out of it, saying I did not want that on my conscience and although I was really upset about everything it was definitely not the right thing to be doing.

Petrified for my life, I thought that every time I left the house someone was going to shoot me. How could what I thought, just a few years ago, was a relatively normal, functional family end up like this?

Chapter 2 – Diagnosis And Cancellation Of Our Holiday

One by one I gave up my cleaning jobs as I was simply becoming incapable of doing them.

On visiting my doctor he told me I was a hypochondriac and looked me up and down as I walked in and incredibly told me to pick my feet up! I told him that I was walking like that because I could not pick my feet up because they were too painful. He told me to stop looking on Google and imagining things that I didn't have. As I did not even own a computer at that time I told him this was impossible for me do but I did know there was something very seriously wrong with me.

It took a few visits to him before he reluctantly agreed to do some blood tests. By this time I was very fatigued and job-wise was only managing a little bit of ironing and the school run. When I rang for the blood results the doctor said my rheumatoid factor was negative but I did have a low thyroid function. I later learned that the rheumatoid factor test is a complete waste of time as it can be negative and the person can have Rheumatoid Arthritis and be positive and the person be very well with nothing wrong with them.

He prescribed some Thyroxin and assured me that after a short period of time I would be feeling back to normal and as fit as a fiddle. Although I was happy with this and trusted him lots of people were telling me that I had too severe symptoms for me to have just a low thyroid. My knowledge of illness was quite limited at this time in my life.

I realised that all through the trauma of my dad's illness, looking after my mum, the fallout and death of my mum, I had soldiered on in spite of the grief and hurt that constantly plagued me. It was obvious that my mind, body and soul needed to rest and recover.

Andrew knew a lovely lady called Dee who I had met a few times at various music events. She was a healer and I rang her for an appointment. She was a lovely, gently-spoken, shy lady who warmly welcomed me in with a hug.

She was deeply shocked to see me hobbling and weak when the last time she had seen me I was dancing and full of energy and vitality.

She did a lot of listening and, like me, agreed that my body had become ill due to all the stress and bad feeling I had gone through.

She did a very strange therapy called cupping on me and said my adrenal glands were not functioning properly. She would also do beautiful guided meditations with me and taught me many relaxation exercises. She gifted me with a juicer and told me various fruits and vegetables that would help me.

All these things helped and she rapidly became my friend and we would often end the sessions in her front room chatting about all sorts of things and drinking herbal teas together.

This, however, was not enough and my pain continued to get worse. I returned to the doctor and insisted he refer me to a rheumatologist which he refused. It was at this point I changed my doctor as I felt my present doctor was not helping me at all and I needed some answers urgently.

My new doctor listened to me and on examining me agreed with me that I definitely needed to see a rheumatologist and referred me straight away.

Six months on from my mum's death I was pretty much bedridden, struggling to do almost everything. Andrew and I went to stay at his parents' house in Ratby, Leicestershire, by which time I was losing weight fast .

His parents were very shocked to see me so thin and weak. They had a wonderful swimming pool and I remember being convinced that even though I could not walk very well I would still be able to swim.

Soon after arriving there I went and got my swimming costume on and came outside with Andrew to have a swim. Andrew's mum, Lilian, was really excited to see this and came out to watch. She and his dad, Alan, had always said they got a lot of enjoyment watching me swim effortlessly up and down their pool.

When I got into the pool and attempted to swim, to my absolute horror, all I could do was flail about trying desperately to keep myself afloat. Lilian who had come out to watch me retreated very quickly into the house, quite obviously embarrassed, shocked and saddened. Not nearly as sad as me. Finding that I could no longer swim I found actually harder than not being able to walk. I had swum since I was a very small child and had my 2 mile badge at the age of 10 and had also gained my bronze life-saving award when I was a young teenager.

Water had always been my solitude and swimming almost came more naturally to me than walking. I was almost an athletic swimmer and had swum in more pools, lakes and rivers than I could even remember. I absolutely adored being in the water and had taught quite a few friends to swim too. And here I was, in a pool, unable to even swim a width. It was completely soul-destroying.

The appointment came to see the rheumatologist and I had my assigned 10 minutes with her and no more. She was a miserable, sour-faced lady without an ounce of compassion.

In the appointment she looked at my joints and informed me that I had Rheumatoid Arthritis and that if I did not take the medication in a year's time I would be totally crippled and in a wheelchair.

She gave me a prescription for Methotrexate and told me to make a further appointment in six month's time to see how I was doing and then ushered me out of the door.

Andrew and I were left standing in the corridor of the hospital in a state of total shock and I must admit I am so grateful that he was there with me.

It made me wonder how many people were cruelly diagnosed with serious and/or terminal illnesses in such a manner, with no kind of counselling, just left to digest the information alone.

Personally I felt like just walking in front of a bus but Andrew assured me that we would come up with a solution and I would get better.

We decided that before going on the Methotrexate (I had been warned that this was a very toxic drug with lots of nasty side-effects) that I should try all the natural avenues, beginning with diet. I knew that there were foods that I should be avoiding and that there were also foods that would help me. With Andrew beside me making plans for a natural recovery I felt slightly better.

Andrew and I had a holiday booked to stay in a hotel in the mountains in Cyprus which we were both looking forward to. When we booked it I was fighting fit so the precautionary note telling us that it was not suitable for people with any kind of mobility issues obviously had not fazed us. In fact I had positively embraced the whole thing. The hotel and surrounding areas were either very steep or had lots of steps.

Realising the predicament I was now in, and not knowing if I was going to be OK, suddenly became very worrying to me. We had already paid the full amount for the holiday which was thousands of pounds. Broaching the subject with Andrew about this, he admitted he had also been worrying about it and that maybe we needed to try to cancel it and get our money back.

On contacting the holiday company we had booked it with they said the only way we could get a refund was by getting a letter from my doctor saying I was unfit to travel. My doctor issued this letter and to our utter amazement we got a full refund bar £100 administration fee.

This really depressed me as I had been really looking forward to going on holiday and visiting a country with Andrew that neither of us had been to before. In my heart and head I was still that fit, adventurous girl I had always been and this just highlighted that things were not looking good.

At this point the reality of my situation hit me and I realised just how ill I was. No quick fix was going to sort me out and I seriously began worrying about money. Andrew had no mortgage but he had made it clear at the start of our relationship that I was to make my own investments and our money was always going to be separate. He was very generous and I'm sure I would have been OK but I also liked my independence.

On divorcing my husband I had bought a tiny cottage in the old town of Eastbourne. Andrew and I had been using this as a weekend retreat and I had let some of my friends use it to get away.

When I purchased this cottage I met a lovely, kind man who was a financial adviser. He advised me that instead of buying one house I should buy five houses with buy-to-let mortgages. He told me this would serve as a really good long-term investment.

At the time this really frightened me and I said I was happy to just have one house with a small mortgage that I could afford. I loved my little 16th century cottage with its little courtyard garden and I was very proud of it. With the money I had from my divorce in the area I was living in I literally could only have bought a very small, cramped flat. Having lived in a three bedroom cottage with my husband with a lovely big garden and a multitude of sheds this was very depressing so to be buying this cute little cottage near the sea was quite a dream.

On purchasing my little cottage I took my financial adviser out to lunch as a thank-you. He had felt sorry for me as I was going through a horrible divorce and my dad, who had always helped me, was suffering the full-blown effects of Alzheimer's at the time. He took me under his wing and helped me through every stage, even recommending which solicitor to use.

On finding myself really ill and worried about money I decided to contact him again for advice. He was really shocked on hearing how ill I was and said he was more than happy to come and visit me. He explained that I could take money out of my house and buy a few flats to rent out and also he suggested that I rent my cottage out.

Although with the mortgages this would not bring me much income he assured me that this would be a good long-term investment. He suggested that I sold the company shares that had been left to me by my parents and invest that money in stocks and shares as they were doing really well at the time.

I followed all of his advice and although due to the property crash I did not make much money on the property miraculously the shares brought me in a satisfactory income for the whole time that I was seriously ill.

This is another of the many blessings I am eternally grateful for. During my time of great need I basically had no money worries.

My uncle Mike and auntie Sylvia who were also my godparents (I call them my Fairy Godparents) said they could be there for anything that needed doing in my house and flats.

Generally, bar a few exceptions, my tenants were good and Mike and Sylvia kept to their word. The tenant that rented my cottage stayed there for seven years before he finally purchased it from me so I was really lucky. When anything was needed, or any decorating needed doing, Mike and Sylvia went over and only ever charged me a very small amount for the work that they carried out.

They are great hoarders and often had what was needed and would then only ask for their travelling expenses. They also helped me at the initial purchase, decorating, choosing carpets and making them presentable to enable me to bring in the highest rent possible.

They were, and are today, my favourite and most loyal of my family and I love and appreciate them more and more with each year. As a child I stayed with them during some of my holidays and always loved being in their home and huge garden. They were always a bit alternative and much more laid-back than my parents and I loved being around them. They look outside the box and have enjoyed a lot of travelling and out of all my family I can relate to them the most.

I am very grateful for all the love and support they have always shown me. My auntie Sylvia always has time for me and we are both there for each other. We mainly talk on the phone, often for hours, and I so appreciate the close friendship we now have as adults.

Chapter 3 - Diet

Andrew and I both researched into how to cure Rheumatoid Arthritis by diet. Andrew stayed up late for many evenings determined he was going to work everything out to make me better. We asked a lot of people and got advice from far and wide.

I started with an elimination diet of all foods, just drinking water. Amazingly, in this time of no food my pain was nearly all gone.

Gradually, one by one, I introduced different foods back into my diet keeping a diary of any effects I felt when I ate them.

I definitely found certain foods — mainly from the nightshade family — increased my pain, particularly potatoes. To not be able to eat potatoes was not going to be easy as they had always been a staple to me and I loved them. I would, however, do ANYTHING to be free of the pain and be free of the living nightmare that had become my life.

Basically, I went on a very strict organic diet cutting out all sugar, white flour and processed food. I put a lot of fresh organic fruit and vegetables through the juicer. Every day I had 8 to 10 carrots, celery, raw beetroot, ginger and an apple to sweeten.

The juicer Dee had given me blew up. My friend Lorraine said she had bought one and it was just sitting in her cupboard and she wasn't likely to use it again so I could have it. With all the use this also blew up too after a short time.

My friend who owned an organic cafe had a Champion juicer which she said, to her knowledge, was the best juicer on the market at that time so I invested in one. It was a good investment as I still have it to this day and I have not even had to replace any of the parts. It is a real work-horse!

On this super diet my hair grew very long, shiny and healthy, my nails were long and strong, my eyesight improved and my skin radiated. My energy levels were slightly improved too. Unfortunately, despite all these health benefits my body remained in excruciating pain. Even having a sheet over me hurt.

I followed this diet strictly for about 2 years but unfortunately this alone was clearly not going to be enough to get me back to optimum health.

Chapter 4 - The Herbalist, Painting And Hydrotherapy

One of Andrew's clients was a Western herbalist with a very good reputation. Before becoming a herbalist he had trained as a doctor and also a surgeon. He did not like the rigidity of conventional medicine so had gone on to study Western herbalism in great detail.

Andrew contacted him and a day was arranged for him to come to give me a consultation. He came and asked a lot of questions about my body and my personal life, both past and present. He asked me about my health as a child and beyond. When I told him that I had had bad eczema as a child he enquired as to what the doctor had treated this with. I told him for most of my childhood I had used Betnovate Cream which was very soothing and helped a lot. I told him it also had a lovely smell to it. When he told me this was a steroid cream and it had now been banned I was really shocked. He was sure that after many years of use that it would have compromised my immune system. He told me that was probably the reason that I had not suffered from any of the normal childhood diseases. And there was me thinking that I was just super healthy! My mum would have been horrified to know this as she did not like taking unnecessary drugs and thought of Betnovate as a pretty harmless cream. My mum would always give me the choice whether I had vaccinations and I know my friends were jealous when they were being made to have jabs and I was opting out of them!

Andrew was answering a lot of the questions for me about my health. The herbalist started asking me more personal questions about my periods and my bowels. I have never had a problem with talking about my bowels but Andrew was finding it quite embarrassing and made his excuses and left. The herbalist told me he had deliberately done this to get rid of him as he really needed to hear the answers from me.

After many hours he finally diagnosed me with Polymyalgia Rheumatica which he said was not as bad as Rheumatoid Arthritis and would more than likely burn itself out within a few years.

By this time I was in excruciating pain throughout my whole body so this was music to my ears that I would one day be well and free of pain again. He was confident that with the right herbal remedies he would get me better and advised me not to take the methatrexate. He told me also that this was highly toxic and would just cause further complications.

Over the next few years I found myself counting the time away waiting for the disease to just disappear. I had heard of this happening and it was a scenario that I waited for with eager anticipation.

Having always been a very "natural" person, even favouring aromatherapy oils over painkillers, this appealed to me a lot. The pain I was experiencing was like no other pain I had ever had so I was more than happy to follow his guidelines, believing that he would get me better. He asked me to get regular blood tests and report them to him and he would adjust the mixture accordingly.

One of the main tests I had done regularly at the hospital was ESR which basically indicates how much inflammation there is in the body. This should be between 1 and 12 and mine was 102! The other blood test that he thought was very indicative of what was happening was the CPR test. This indicates the reaction in the body and that too was incredibly high. Before he left me that first time he told me that I needed to release some of my anger and suggested I did some painting using red and black paints.

On his instructions I went out and bought some watercolour paints and paper. Having never been an artist and being told at school I was useless, I did not expect any great works of art.

Sitting at the dining-room table I was struggling to even hold the paintbrush as my fingers, hands and wrists hurt so much but I persevered hoping that by the end of it I would feel better and I would have released some of the anger that was buried inside me.

Having never used watercolours before, I was surprised and delighted at the effect the paint made on the watered paper. I was not feeling any particular anger at the time but did as instructed. I just used red and black paints on a large piece of paper. The result was rather pleasing and looked like a sea of abstract fish. I was so happy with it that I cut the paper into 3 pieces and found 3 frames and framed them. Finding myself on a roll at this point I started to do other abstract paintings which looked like planets and they too, much to my surprise, were pretty amazing.

A few days later my friends Laura and Andy came round and Andy asked me about the red and black paintings and where they had come from. He said he loved them and asked if he could purchase them. He gave me £30 for them … WOW. I had not expected that! This boosted my confidence and a new-found hobby began. I went on to sell about another 50 paintings and gave many away as gifts.

It was nice at Christmas to be able to give friends and family something personal as getting to the shops had become nigh on impossible. My friends were quite clearly impressed with them and I also went on to give away more to people that helped me out over the coming years as a thank you. I gave a huge one to my financial adviser as he had admired them when he came to my house. It was a nice thing to be doing and everyone was so appreciative. Andrew and I managed to purchase a job lot of new frames from a charity shop so none of it cost me very much which was a bonus.

In the meantime I was taking my herbal tincture daily and the blood tests were very slowly coming down although by this time I was not only in excruciating pain, I was also incredibly fatigued.

From having spent so much time in bed, my muscles were wasting away. I was finding I was sleeping more and more, to the point where I would only be awake for meals and visits to the toilet. I would often wake up hoping it was all a nightmare. I never knew it was possible for someone to sleep for such long periods of time and still be tired. Often I would awake thinking surely I cannot still be in bed and then as soon as I had thought it I would drift off again. It had got to the point where I was either asleep or totally exhausted and always in a lot of pain.

The old stables we lived in was not like the standard accommodation with living rooms on the ground floor and bedrooms upstairs. The ground floor consisted of a large kitchen, Andrew's workshop and office with a toilet off the workshop. Upstairs was our dining room, a large music room/lounge and our bedroom was at the back. The dining room and music room were large, light, airy rooms with the bedroom being small and quite dark at the back of the house with a small window which did not let in a great deal of light. When I had been well, the set-up worked wonderfully and I loved our little snuggly bedroom. Finding myself as good as bedridden with not much to look at was making me very depressed.

Although Andrew loved the music room he did agree that it would be better for me if we converted that into our bedroom. Our original bedroom had a fitted wardrobe that he had built so we now needed a wardrobe in the big room. We went to the local antique shop and I fell in love with a French oak wardrobe with green glass panels. Andrew gave me some money towards it and we had it delivered to our house,

This room had floor-to-ceiling windows and I could see a bit of the outside world. It also had amazing vaulted ceilings which I adored. This meant I could now look out of the window and feel the space all around me as I lay in bed. It felt less oppressive being in that room and my mood lifted considerably. Looking back on that time it was the best room in which I could have spent being in bed practically solidly for 4 years.

Obviously I am aware that within the horror that my life had become I did have many, many blessings. The hospital at this point arranged for me to have some hydrotherapy. I nervously went along and connected immediately with Jackie, the physio/hydrotherapist. She was a keen swimmer herself and we were about the same age so we could relate to a lot of things together.

Most people in the pool were very relieved when their 20 minutes were up but I felt devastated to be getting out of the comfort of the beautiful warm pool. Here I could move so much more easily and could even walk properly. It struck me how "normal" we all looked in the pool compared to outside the pool. At best people were on sticks but most in wheelchairs. Not only did I look more normal but more importantly I felt more normal. This was a very natural familiar environment for me and I felt totally at home and relaxed. Jackie recognised this and ended up, after a while, just letting me stay in the corner of the pool, exercising while everyone came and went. Sometimes I would be in there for way over an hour. In the end I would phone Andrew when I was ready as he never knew what time to collect me as it was getting later and later. When I did get home I would be exhausted but so much happier for having exercised. I loved the ache that came from exercise, rather than the normal achy pains I was used to.

I connected with many people in a deep and meaningful way in that pool. There was one particular lady who stands out to me. She was suffering from MS and had spent a good few years in a wheelchair. She had the best sense of humour I have ever witnessed and she was the life and soul of the pool. She would have the staff and patients in fits of laughter every week. She really was a breath of fresh air to us all and lifted our spirits. She was using cannabis for pain relief and quite often she would be stoned and her laugh was very infectious. I would often spend time chatting and laughing with her in the changing rooms and we would often chat while we were both waiting for our lifts to turn up. She was a very sociable lady and a lot of fun.

Sadly, much later on, I was to learn that she had committed suicide. It was as if her huge personality just could not fit the disabled life she was living. Jackie often used to try and persuade her to do some hospital radio work as she had such a great sense of humour and would come across really well on the radio. Unfortunately she never did this and I think it is a shame as it would have given her a focus and built up her confidence.

Listening to the local news one day I was pleased to hear that her brother was present at the time of her passing so she did not die alone and had someone she loved holding her hand as she passed away. He ended up in court for assisting a person in dying but fortunately he was cleared.

There was also a lady I liked a lot who had lost a leg in an accident at the age of 10. She had grown up and had gone on to get married and have a child. She and her husband loved caravanning and at every opportunity they were away enjoying themselves. She always appeared happy and was a true inspiration to me. Seeing her happy made me think that I too could be happy. She took great pride in her appearance and like me her favourite colour was purple. She had beautiful manicured and painted finger nails and always looked a million dollars,

Some of the things I saw in that pool saddened me greatly — adults and children that had been in dreadful accidents or had had severe strokes. These people would be stretchered in by a nurse from the ward and then hoisted in.

Jackie was just amazing with these people, treating them with so much respect and compassion. I would just look on in awe of the amazing job she was doing. She then went on to train in Watsu and asked if I would be her guinea pig which I jumped at. These sessions were incredible and evoked a memory of being in the womb. It involved her holding and rocking and stretching me in the warm water. During this I was held against her with my ears just below the water. She rocked me from side-to-side and it was incredibly relaxing. During this session I could hear her heartbeat and it left me in a calm, comforted and content state of being.

To this day I feel truly blessed for all the experiences I had in that pool and for all the beautiful people I met there. There were a lot of humbling lessons learnt.

These sessions were on the NHS and eventually came to an end as, due to cutbacks, they had been restricted to a maximum of six weeks. I had been lucky as I had been going for a number of months.

Jackie told me about an arthritis hospital that had a hydrotherapy pool where I could pay for a consultation. If they were confident I was safe in the water I could then join in with the group sessions, which were only £5.00 for half an hour.

Pulling into the hospital was quite depressing as it was clearly marked as an arthritic hospital, another reminder of where I was in my life. The consultant was lovely and after a session he said he was happy for me to join the group sessions. Everyone was older than me and had become friends and I felt quite left out. Knowing that I was primarily there to exercise I found a corner where I did my exercises. Looking out the window there was a wood and as I marched on the spot I imagined myself walking through the woods. People in the pool ignored me if I tried to join in their conversations and I felt unwelcome and uncomfortable. One of the physiotherapist's assistants took me to one side as she had watched what was happening and suggested I came on another day. She said the day I came was very cliquey and on the other day everyone that attended was much nicer, had a laugh and were really good fun. She said she preferred working that day as it was a better atmosphere. I thanked her and changed my day. She was right and I started looking forward to these afternoons. I attended these for a good few years and made some beautiful friendships with both the patients and staff. Sometimes I would pay for double or even triple sessions and as I got to know the staff they would often just wink at me to stay in there.

One of the physiotherapists, Chris, was about my age and I bonded with her straight away as we had a lot in common. She was a shopaholic and asked me if I was aware of Shopmobility and I said no. She said she was happy to pick me up and take me to Crawley where I could hire a scooter to get around the shops. I was initially very nervous but she came with me and once I had mastered these scooters I realised it was a lot of fun. Boy did she teach me how to shop!

From then on we made these trips quite regularly and looked around the shops, had lunch and we had a really good laugh together too. A lot of my friends, even if they visited, didn't like the idea of taking me out so these trips were a real lifeline and very much appreciated. She also had a cabriolet car with heated seats and she was more than happy to help me in and out of it. We became really good friends and I will always appreciate what she did for me. She helped build my confidence, which I was losing by the day. Being in pain and incapable of most things can be completely soul-destroying. When new people I met liked me and wanted to be in my company it was proof that I was still worthy even though I felt useless.

The hospital also sent me on an occupational therapy course which was to last 6 weeks. Partners were encouraged to attend with the patients but Andrew said he did not have the time or inclination to come with me. Everyone else had their partners with them and to be honest I found it a bit of a "pity party" with everyone whingeing about their lives. I was the only person not taking the conventional drugs and was greatly scoffed at for thinking I could cure myself naturally.

Although I probably ended up with a lot more damage with the decisions I made I cannot regret those decisions as that is what I strongly believed in at the time and believed that the drugs would kill me. This was therefore the only journey I could have made. If I hadn't I would have spent my life wondering what could have been. I guess at this point too I was in denial of what was really happening and did not realise fully what the consequences were if my plan did not work. I was used to being fit and athletic and refused to believe that I could be permanently disabled.

There were some useful tips on how to manage tasks differently and I realised that there is more than one way to get results and as long as you reach your goal it matters not how you get there. There were also some nice guided meditations that were very relaxing and sometimes some nice relaxing music was played.

An occupational therapist arranged to come to our house to assess me. She was a bit shocked at how disabled unfriendly it was with its steep drive, steps at the front and back and our steep staircase inside.

She provided me with a Zimmer frame/chair with a compartment underneath to carry things from the bedroom to the bathroom. She also provided a chair that enabled me to easily put my head over the sink so someone could wash my hair, and a board across the bath so I could get into the bath to stand up under the shower. Getting in and out of the bath by this time had become impossible. She gave me a raised toilet seat which was brilliant as I now did not have to dangerously throw myself down on to the toilet and it was easier to get up off the toilet too. All these things were appreciated. She also arranged for a chiropodist to visit and cut my toe nails. She recommended that we pay for a carer to come in and help as Andrew was obviously struggling to work, do all the housework, cook and look after me as well.

We hired Pat who turned out to be an absolute star. She would come in once a week and do all the things that needed doing. Andrew hated ironing so she would do that, change the bed and wash my hair and try and keep my spirits up. It was incredible what she managed to do in a very short amount of time and it took a lot of pressure off Andrew.

It was nice to have some regular female company and she was a kindly motherly type woman. She had grown up daughters and she would talk about her life and her family and the wonderful cruises she went on with her husband. She would show me photos of the cruises and it was surprising to see the glamorous pictures of her all dressed and made up. The lady I knew wore a drab uniform, her hair was grey and she looked pretty dull most of the time. It was very insightful to see that she was so much more than this. It was nice to hear her stories of other peoples lives and what they were all up to.

She also talked about other people she helped, some of whom were a lot worse than me. She talked of hoists and catheters and the many people involved in the looking after of these poor people. She and the consultant both implied that this was going to happen to me in the near future. Andrew admitted to me that he felt he could not cope with me at home if all this happened and we would have to look at alternatives.

I found these conversations very distressing and depressing and refused to be drawn into them. I had an inner feeling that some kind of miracle would happen before this scenario. The thought of being catheterised at home was unbearable to me. Pat said it wasn't a problem and she was OK with coming in and emptying the bag. I raised my voice and said, "It bothers me and it's not going to happen!" She said it was an inevitability and I was never going to have a normal life again. I calmly told her that I was not going to argue with her, that I was going to get better and live an independent life again. She looked very sorry for me and said maybe I needed to be a bit more realistic. We agreed to disagree and she started to do the ironing. Things went back to how they were and there was no more mention of hoists or catheters!

Dee would still ring me from time to time to see how I was doing. She had never taken on board my diagnosis and was still convinced I did not have Rheumatoid Arthritis.

During the conversation I told her I was depressed as it was autumn and I was stuck in bed and wanted to be outside kicking leaves as I had always done. She told me I could still do this but in my mind. She told me to picture it, imagine it and enjoy it. That particular day I was feeling churlish and said it was hardly the same but when I came off the phone to her I did actually do it and found it was better than sulking! She told me that she had heard of a homeopath that had a diagnostic machine and she thought I should go and see her.

On obtaining her number I rang her and arranged an appointment at her clinic.

Chapter 5 - Homeopathy, Suicidal Thoughts And Angels

Having made the appointment to see the homeopath I went to her house, which was a large Sussex farmhouse with an outbuilding set up as her clinic. She came outside and invited me in and I sat down. She asked me a lot of questions and once again the Betnovate cream came up. She told me that she thought because I remembered the smell so well and remembered it with such fondness her guess was that I had become addicted to it.

On telling her that I was adopted she became quite animated. She asked me if I knew of the book The Primal Wound. I said I had never heard of it and she said it was very important for me to read and understand the meaning of it. I did read this book as she requested and at the time was not overly impressed with it but have since read it again and it makes perfect sense to me now but that subject would take up another book!

She told me that a great many of her patients were adopted and, in later life, became ill because of the primal wound and, never seeking any help, found themselves unable to cope with their life. She asked me how I was with rejection and, on thinking about this, I realised that any kind of rejection I had had in my life I had taken really badly whether it had been a boy I liked ignoring me, relationship breakdowns or being turned down for a job. This is something I have put a lot of thought into and it makes me understand myself a lot better and how I have reacted to many things throughout my entire life. My adopted mother basically rejected me in the end, or at least that is how it felt, and that had most definitely contributed to me being ill. It was most definitely an interesting subject!

She then asked me to put a helmet on my head which had wires coming out of it which she connected to a computer. She told me that this would clearly diagnose me and tell her what homeopathic remedies would cure me.

She did not follow the standard practice and used a lot of very expensive German tinctures. I ended up very very ill under her, not only having severe mobility issues but also having a fever and really bad night sweats.

Andrew was very worried about me and voiced his fears to her but she assured him that I had to get worse to get better and that was the way of homeopathy.

Unfortunately I just got worse and worse and was in such a bad way that she started to come to me, giving me new things to try. Everything she gave me made me worse. I got so bad that I didn't even feel human anymore. I felt like a wrung-out dishcloth.

The last time she came she did seem very baffled and looked very worried. I sensed that she was now just stabbing in the dark not knowing what she was doing or the effect it was going to have on me. Her original self-assured confidence in curing me was gone. She said she would take a painting instead of payment as she no longer wanted to charge me. She had admired my paintings on the way in as they were stacked up along the wall. After she had chosen a painting she left, clutching it under her arm.

The following week I rang her and told her that I no longer wanted her help. The relief in her voice was audible and it was very obvious that she was in way past her depth.

She never followed it up with a phone call and as far as she was concerned I could have been dead. Andrew was very upset at how unprofessional she was and the fact that she never once apologised. I think she was scared and ran away and I can kind of understand that but I think I am more forgiving than Andrew.

By this time I was very depressed and my life seemed like it had been completely taken away from me. Every single day was now spent in bed, all day, mainly sleeping. When I wasn't sleeping I would be struggling to get to the toilet. Finishing on the toilet I would remain sat on the toilet for ages because it was too painful to get up and then I would struggle back to bed. If we did go out anywhere, which was mainly just appointments now, it would take me 45 minutes to get from my bedroom to the car. I started to believe that my life was not worth living and that if I just took an overdose all my pain would be over. It felt like I was only alive for other people as I knew my death would be very upsetting but it was my life and it was horrendous. Obviously I did not want anybody blaming themselves so I told Andrew and a few of my dearest friends of my intentions. This was extremely upsetting but I think they understood and Andrew said if I was going to do it, to make sure that I did it properly. He did not want me suffering any more and did not want to be caring for me with additional problems, ie liver failure.

My mind was pretty much made up when I had an experience that would completely change my way of thinking and give me hope.

I woke up in the middle of the night and, although it was pitch dark, I could see what I can only describe as bright silver lights all over the ceiling. My bedroom had very high vaulted ceilings and these lights were all over it. These lights were a tadpole type shape. Before I knew it I found myself looking down from the ceiling at my body on the bed. I was being held in massive wings as I watched my physical body being massaged and very gently and lovingly caressed by several angels. They had the most beautiful elegant hands and fingers imaginable. It seemed that this went on for a long time before I was gently lowered down "into my body". The only way I can describe this was like a feeling of being "tucked into bed". I felt completely serene, calm, free of any pain and had a very strong feeling that I was going to be all right. At that moment I was aware that I was a precious being and greatly loved.

I went into a deep slumber, awakening in the morning remembering very clearly everything that had happened. I thought "Wow, I must have been healed". But alas, on moving all the excruciating pain was still there. That was obviously a blow to me but the feeling that I was going to be OK stayed with me very strongly and I never ever have debated suicide again.

Andrew bumped into an artist friend of ours, Kate, at the local organic food shop and she enquired after me. She knew I had not been well as her son had done some work for Andrew in his school holidays for some cash. Andrew told her how ill I was and that I was mainly confined to bed and in a lot of pain.

She did a lot of artwork in churches, on walls and ceilings and was very talented at what she did. I had once been to her house and admired some of her paintings and knew her work to be very good.

She told Andrew she had a painting she had done of Angel Gabriel and she felt it should be with me. She thought it would bring me comfort. She told

Andrew that if he paid a nominal amount of money for the cost of the materials he could take it home for me. He paid the money, collected it and, much to my delight, brought it home. We propped it up on the wall opposite my bed so I could look at it all the time. I found looking at it so peaceful and healing and I was really happy this beautiful painting was there in front of me. Right up to to this day it is one of my most treasured possessions and still has pride of place in my home. Most people that come to our home comment on it and say they can feel the healing energy coming from it. It alternates between our living room and the bedroom depending on my health and mood. Most of our pictures are changed around regularly as I believe by doing this our home does not become stagnant and remains interesting. I find it a bit disturbing when I go to peoples houses and every single ornament, plant and item of furniture remains in the exact same place sometimes for decades. We are all different and I understand that there is probably comfort there for these people but I, personally, feel that variety is the spice of life.

One day I was lying in bed in more pain than usual and my mobile phone rang. I struggled to pick it up as I could hardly use my hands or arms. It was my dear friend Ken on the line, very excited and speaking very fast, saying he had had a sign that I was going to be OK.

After asking him to slow down, he explained that someone had come into his shop very upset that someone in their family had been diagnosed with Rheumatoid Arthritis. He started to tell her about me and how depressed he was as he believed I would be crippled for life. Suddenly, he told me, he felt overwhelmed with peace and what he described could only have been an angelic presence. He felt uplifted and heard himself telling the woman, with great conviction, that I was going to be OK. He said that these words just tumbled out of his mouth without him having thought them first. When the lady left the shop he rang me immediately, totally elated, and had to tell me that he absolutely knew with all his heart and soul that I was going to recover. Being in so much pain at the time, barely even able to hold my phone, I was not elated as he had expected me to be and not very convinced either and cannot even remember what my response was. I think it was probably abrupt, and sadly have to admit that pain sometimes did not make me into the nicest of friends. There were times, at my lowest, when I totally resented everyone getting on with their lives while I just laid in bed in pain or asleep.

Obviously with hindsight there were many signs of angels around me and I now don't doubt what he told me on the phone that day and I think on some subconscious level that the message did filter through.

Chapter 6 - Bowen Therapy

Dee rang me one day and I told her that I was now completely bed-ridden and very very ill. She said she could hear how ill I was by the weakness and dullness of my voice and was very worried about me. She, herself, had suffered from an auto immune disease and always claimed that she was lucky to be alive so was only too aware of how ill I could become.

My herbalist had always claimed that a lot of his diagnosis of a persons health was based on their voice. When I thought about this — and old people — I had known their voices had become feeble along with their bodies.

Dee had recently heard of a man called Alistair Rattray, who was becoming very well known for his Bowen Therapy. She asked me if I wanted her to ring him and see if he would come and see me. She did ring him but he said he only really dealt with asthma clients and people who were terminally ill and that he was too busy. Bless Dee, she said he MUST come and visit me and obviously got over the urgency of my situation to him as he agreed to come. She arranged a date and time for him to visit me for a consultation and treatment and rang me back with the news. She said that he had such a good reputation and she was confident he would be able to help me.

Alistair arrived as planned and Andrew let him in. Andrew chatted to him for a long time in the kitchen. Andrew told me later that he fully trusted him straight away. He could tell he was very professional and caring and honest.

He came upstairs, knocked on my bedroom door, put his head around the door and asked me if it was OK to come in. He initially sat on a chair opposite the bed. He was a lovely, fatherly-type figure who asked me loads of questions and looked at my joints, making lots of notes as he went along.

He told me that as well as being a Bowen therapist and teacher he had also been a physiotherapist which instilled more faith in me.

He went on to explain what Bowen was, where it had originated from, what it was about and the theory behind how it worked. It was invented by a man called Tom Bowen who was very good at recognising changes in the body — however subtle — and therefore was good at seeing what worked and what didn't. It involves the movement of soft tissue and the move is done with the thumbs and forefingers being rolled over the skin. The idea of this movement is to stimulate the tissue and nerve pathways creating a focus for the brain. Between each movement the therapist takes a break for the brain to process what has happened. He told me that even though he was doing the therapy it would be my body and brain doing the work. For this reason the breaks were possibly the most important part while my body remembered how it should be.

The basic function of the brain is receiving information from our sensory organs and interpreting that information such as sound, light and movement. The brain is able to adjust its response to new situations and this includes touch. There are hundreds and thousands of signals that travel from the brain into the body every single second and these in turn come back to the brain with information which it interprets and sends back. Whenever we sense or even think something the brain brings in past experience in order to understand and create a response. In the case of the

Bowen moves the brain does not instantly receive the signals and needs more information. When the therapist leaves the room the brain sends specific signals to the area to gain a response. Often that response is quick and results in deep relaxation. It is a hard therapy to understand as the therapist himself does not actually do very much. At first my reaction was that it felt like a bit of a rip-off for that reason. As my body responded I began to realise the benefits of the whole procedure. Often Alistair would come and only do the most minimal of movements and that would be a whole session. It is a great treatment as, if it doesn't work, there is no harm done but if it does work, and the body responds, it can and will repair itself.

He told me he was so relieved that I had told the homeopathy lady I did not want to see her anymore as it was quite clear from what Andrew and I had said I was going "South". I had not heard this expression before and found it quite humorous.

Another thing that I really liked about Bowen was that it was a non-invasive, holistic therapy and I did not have to take any of my clothes off. The idea, Alistair told me, was to get my brain and body to repair and reset itself.

During that first visit I cried a lot, sometimes uncontrollably. Telling him everything kind of brought the reality home to me of how ill I actually was and how far removed I was from my former happy-go-lucky self. Lying there, hardly able to move, talking to a stranger felt quite distressing. It worried me that he would think of me as over-emotional and possibly even a bit mad but he was so empathetic and I think from that very first day a friendship was born.

He did a Bowen therapy on me and when he left I did feel a bit better. Over time I realised, for myself, that it was a necessary and a very beneficial therapy for me and began to understand the importance of the breaks too. Out of all the natural therapies I still say that this was the best for me and I still benefit greatly when I treat myself to one.

Alistair told me that generally people only needed 6 sessions but he felt I was going to need more. He told me to ring him if I was experiencing any problems and he would me more than happy to talk me through them and that was part of his service to me. He said that after the first 6 he would not charge me but would keep coming for as long as was needed. Unable to accept this we came to a price that we could both agree on. He was travelling 10 miles to my house so to not be charged would have been wrong. Alistair was truly an angel sent to me (and Andrew) at possibly the worst time in my life. He would arrive at our house and spend about an hour talking to Andrew downstairs and then come and talk to me and then do the therapy. And talk to me afterwards too. After that he would go downstairs and talk to Andrew again before leaving. He was basically a lifeline, a friend, a counsellor and a therapist to both of us and I'm eternally grateful to him for his unconditional kindness. The amount of time he spent with both of us was far beyond what you would expect from anyone, his time is one of the best gifts I have ever been given. He also had a wonderful sense of humour and despite the pain I was in, we would often be found giggling together.

He persuaded me to at least take the anti-inflammatories prescribed to me as all my joints were severely swollen. I agreed to this and started taking them.

After each treatment Alistair would encourage me to move as much as I could. After one of these treatments he helped me up and started to help me to walk. He was telling me where to put my feet and I realised, with horror, that he was actually teaching me how to walk. My body had forgotten how to do the simplest of tasks. My hands could not move hardly at all and he gave me a soft orange ball to try and squeeze to build up the muscles that I had lost. He also gave me 2 golf balls to roll under my feet to try and improve movement. His previous physiotherapist knowledge was being used as well as his Bowen skills.

Many years later I went to see him and I was laughing with him about how he would finish our sessions by pulling my big toe. We would joke together that it would be a new move that would be the cure for Rheumatoid Arthritis. He became serious and said that he had become very fond of me over the months he spent with me and he really had tried to find a way to rid me of my pain. It pained him to watch me in so much pain and not be able to give me more relief. He really is one of the nicest, kindest people I have had the honour to meet. We remain friends to this day and I have a lot of love in my heart for him and the deepest of respect for the integrity, passion and love he shows within his work.

Chapter 7 - Lotions, Potions and the Weird and Wonderful

Living in an alternative area there were so many people telling me of cures and miracles that were happening all around them and people were forever cutting out articles from papers and magazines of the new miracle that would cure me. It was a very Steiner-based area and I had made quite a few friends within the Steiner community and they recommended a lady to me who did something called rhythmic massage. I had never heard of this but within this community she was held in high regard. Through rhythmical massage there is an attempt and aim to improve the connection of soul and spirit to the physical body. My friends felt that this was what I needed and she would help me. She worked from home and I booked an appointment with her.

She was a no-nonsense German lady who insisted that I make a commitment to her by paying up-front for 10 sessions. The only reason that I could have for not attending was if I was menstruating and then I would have to rest. Any other non-attendance, for whatever reason, would not be refunded. She then asked me, or rather told me, to "strip down to your panties and bra". She then asked me in her very strong German accent how my "vwarms" were. I had to ask her several times what she meant and she shouted at me, "Are you a hot or cold person?" I replied that I did suffer from the cold and she promptly went into a rage about my panties not being cotton. She told me I needed to wear big panties and all-natural clothing which was to be layered. She told me if I did not comply with this she would not treat me again. She then informed me of the procedure she would be doing each week. I would come in, strip to my bra and panties, she would do a massage, cover me and leave me. When I was ready to go I would leave the money on the table and close the door behind me! The massage was lovely with beautiful warming oils and then she put warmed (from the radiator) organic cotton socks on my feet and then a warmed sheet and then several blankets. As she had told me she would, at this point she left the room.

I must admit I did not warm to this lady and her brusque manner but I trusted in my friends that she was good at her job and would therefore get me better. To be honest I think the feeling was mutual and she did not like me either.

The following week I returned having purchased some huge cotton knickers and wearing knitted cotton trousers and various cotton tops. Each week was the same with her disappearing at the end, leaving me struggling to get dressed, off the couch and out the door. There did not seem to be an ounce of compassion in her.

Just before the end of these sessions my Steiner friends suggested I ask her about Park Atwood hospital, which is Steiner-based with qualified doctors to look after you. As well as the basic care there are a lot of Steiner-based therapies including art and Eurythmy. When I used to pick Yvonne's children up from The Michael Hall Steiner school I would see the children and teachers practising Eurythmy. They would all be prancing freely about in what looked like coloured net curtains. Yvonne's eldest child hated it as she felt very self-conscious but although I found it quite funny I could see that it probably was very therapeutic. This school was spiritually and ideologically about a million miles away from my upbringing.

I had attended a very big, rough comprehensive school. I had had to learn to be tough, fight my own battles and become street-wise to survive. If someone had asked me if my spiritual needs were being met I would not have even known what they were talking about! These pupils are even given the choice of whether or not to attend lessons and whether to wear uniform. Their education is based around their emotional and spiritual development. It focuses on the child holistically; the mind body and spirit. They focus on the child's needs at every stage learning through movement and play to make sense of the world around them. A child will have the same teacher all through school to create a bond and knowledge of each other. There is a lot of drama singing and playing of instruments and regular performances. Being around these people made me feel like I had been quite deprived as I know I would have benefitted greatly from this kind of schooling and would have thrived.

School bored me and the subjects were taught in a monotonous way and my mind wandered. Lessons became tedious and one by one I started to bunk off them and in the end I just started to skive off school completely. The teachers seemed quite happy that I was not in their lessons as I had become quite disruptive and naughty. Amazingly I got away with hardly attending school at all for the last year without any repercussions. I would keep my lunch and bus fares and was by then working for the local cobbler having taken on all his hand stitching. The money was great but looking back it was not the life I should have been leading. Not one teacher ever approached me to get to the bottom of my lack of attendance and it was clear that they saw it as a simple solution to a problem so they were happy to just ignore the situation. Seeing these people around me now with their fully rounded education behind them and their many talents did make me start wondering about alternative education. I think that the State schools have got even worse and the curriculum is so rigid. My step-son has so much homework and is often feeling under pressure with numerous exams. His spiritual development is not considered. Luckily, he seems to get on with it and is coping but some of the other children quite clearly are not.

Being around these people was like a breath of fresh air and they were not like anybody I had ever come across in my life before. I was in awe of their life styles and how they seemed to earn large amounts of money without actually doing very much. One of the men I met did therapy with special needs children and charged £50 an hour. I watched him working in a garden one afternoon. His only prop was a brightly-coloured knitted ball. For the whole hour he just played catch. Nice work if you can get it!!

On studying these people closely over the years I lived there I came to the conclusion that there was somehow a big pot of money that just flowed between them. It seemed that it was impossible to get to this flow of money without having had the whole education and belief system in place. These Steiner folk were lovely people and were our friends and we were invited to concerts, markets, recitals and parties and although I loved them and enjoyed time in their company I was always aware I was different to them and would never properly fit into their group. Strangely, they seemed as intrigued by my life and the stories I told them of my home town Redhill. They thought it was all exciting and even tried to tell me they were not really Steiner, it was their parents that were. It was obvious that they were as everything about them screamed Steiner and of course they are now parents sending their children to the same school. And why wouldn't they? It is the best schooling I know of.

When I asked the massage lady about the hospital she appeared very shocked and asked me how I knew about it. I told her that my friends had told me. She said it really was a great place with fine results but would not be for me. She informed me that it would be a waste of my time and money as I would fall flat on my face when I returned home!

This proved my theory, that I could never fully fit into this community and I felt quite hurt and insulted but in reality maybe she was right and like all Steiner things it would have cost what I considered to be a huge amount of money. I left her house never to return.

A friend of ours, Anita, heard about my illness and recommended that I go to her local spiritualist church in Hailsham for some healing. There were healers who were at the church every Tuesday afternoon and were there for anyone who needed healing. All they asked was a small donation to the church.

Andrew and I went along and I was taken into a back room where there was a massage couch and 2 or 3 women healers. They told me to lie down, relax and imagine I was somewhere nice. They placed their hands on and above my body as I just lay still for about half an hour, sometimes an hour, if I was the only person there.

Andrew and I visited here most Tuesdays for a long time and we got to know these lovely people quite well. There was always a man in the main part of the church serving drinks and cake and Andrew always joked with him that he was only there for the cake. My diet, unfortunately, restricted me from this but Andrew always said the cake was very good.

The ladies were always very sympathetic and I would often spend my time with them crying. They were very encouraging and said that with everything that was happening to me I needed to cry. I hate crying in front of people but these ladies were older and very motherly and I found them very comforting and supportive. I am not entirely sure that the healing itself did much for me but these lovely ladies took the time out of their lives to show love and care towards me, which was very heart-warming and touched my soul deeply. To me anyone who takes time to help and comfort strangers are angels and we all need such people at one time or another. I am always touched by people's compassion and kindness and these are the best qualities any human being can possess.

To any of you reading this that take time out to help others, you are angels and I send my love and blessings out to you all.

The next thing to be recommended to me was an incredible spiritual healer who would be attending a local church and doing "miraculous" free healing on people. Of course, being in the dreadful state I was in, this was a very appealing ideal to me. I needed a miracle in my life!

We went along and watched the spectacle that was to follow. Andrew and I arrived early and sat at the front. The healer's wife came around with a book asking who would like healing, writing down their names and the condition that needed attention. She asked what was wrong with me and I told her I had Rheumatoid Arthritis. She had seen me hobbling when I came in and could see that I was in a lot of pain and in desperate need of a miracle. She was very sympathetic and said she really hoped that I was chosen and he would heal me.

Andrew mentioned that it would be good if he could sort out his knees that were suffering from long-term Morris dancing. She told him that he was very good at operating on these kinds of problems with excellent results. Andrew said to me that he would rather I was called up than him and that was our reason for being there.

The church slowly filled up with a lot of people, many of whom were clearly very sick and in need of a miracle. I am sure some just came for the entertainment! The spiritual healer/psychic surgeon got up and introduced himself and explained what was going to happen throughout the evening.

He said he would go into a deep trance and soon after that his body would be completely taken over by his guide who had lived over 2000 years ago. He would (allegedly) randomly call people from the list and said he would be operating on them as he could see inside the body to all the muscles, tissues and organs. Eventually he went into a meditative-like state and then he started talking slightly differently and this was (apparently) the guide doctor. He called quite a few people up including Andrew. He "operated" on Andrew's knees and there were lots of jokes and laughter about the Morris dancing. The whole thing was quite a show and Andrew took full advantage of this, asking if he could operate on his neck and wrists too.

It was very hands-on, with a lot of bone-crunching and Andrew reported later that it was like having a heavy-handed osteopath work on him admittedly with great results. Everybody else that was called up seemed to also benefit greatly from these "operations".

After working on these people he said he was tired and had to go and the original man came back looking quite vacant.

He said he was sorry if his guide had not come to people that desperately needed healing but he did various clinics that we could attend and there was a leaflet giving details with the times they would be there if we wanted to pick one up on the way out. They were drop-in clinics so no need to book, just turn up and wait your turn. We picked up a leaflet on the way out and of course I wanted to go as what I had seen was a lot of people being healed.

Their nearest clinic was about 20 miles away and was on a Saturday so we made the journey the following week. We sat in a full waiting room with many excited people who could not wait to have their ailments "cured". Many people had read or heard about him and were happy to pay money for the healing. The charges were what you would have expected for any other therapy so I would imagine that he was on a good wage as it worked out about £80 an hour. We were given a ticket with a number on and when our number was called we were to go through to the next room.

The psychic surgeon was already "there" in the man's body and carried out many operations throughout the morning, seeing all the people in the waiting room. I can remember wondering why he was not getting tired as he had in the spiritualist church but did not let my thoughts dwell on it as I too wanted a miracle to occur and to get my life back.

When it was my turn I was called into the other room and he was behind a curtain with a computer and a massage couch. He took down all my details on his computer also making a note of what he had done at the end of the "operation". He went through my joints manipulating them with a lot of very scary crunching noises. This was quite painful but bearable. He then sat me up and did my back and neck. He told me to keep coming back and each time I would feel a little bit better. He said it could be a long process.

He asked me to pay his wife on the way out. His wife also had postcards that a psychic artist had done of the guide who had lived in the time of Jesus . She said this guide had chosen her husband to take over his body so he could help anyone in need. It was a far-fetched story but it is quite incredible what you will believe when you are desperate and in pain. Looking back it really was all about hope, as long as I could focus on getting better and keep that hope alive life was worth living. For that reason I thank every one of these people whether they were for real or not for allowing me hope, which was without a doubt in a very hard period of my life.

She recommended buying one of these postcards and keeping it by my bed so I could call on him for healing and then she suggested that maybe I buy one for my handbag too! Believe it or not I actually bought 2 and in bad times I did pray to them!

There is a lot of power in prayer I think. When the body and mind are screaming out for help that is a release in itself and a surrender to something bigger and more powerful than you. This postcard did actually help me at the time.

My posture was considerably better and my walking slightly better but this only lasted for a few days. We religiously returned each week with the same bone crunching manipulations and the same results lasting for just a short time.

By this time Andrew had developed a heart problem and had a leaky mitral valve so he decided to pay for an appointment too. The healer told him he needed to go to the hospital and have it x-rayed. I wondered again at his authenticity as he had originally claimed, in the church, that he could see everything in the body.

The time came for Andrew to have a heart operation and the guide told him that everything would be OK as he would be overseeing the operation and guiding the surgeon. The operation had its problems as it was supposed to be to repair the valve but that was not successful so they then had to replace it with a mechanical one. This was a major heart operation and obviously took a lot longer than was anticipated. Every time I rang the hospital I was told he was still not out and there had been a problem but they did not know what it was. My God-Parents had come to stay with me as they knew it would be a difficult day and they were trying their best to keep me distracted but as time went on I could not think of anything else. To make matters worse I had his mum keep ringing me to see if he was out of the operation. In the end we agreed that I would ring her the moment I knew anything. Eventually the operation was over and they said he was OK but was in intensive care so they could closely monitor him. I was worried what his reaction was going to be when he came round hearing that he had a replacement rather than a repair. A friend of his had had one many years ago and it ticked like a clock and kept him awake.

I rang his mum and reassured her as best as I could that he was OK. The next day he was taken down to the ward and my friend took me to see him. He was covered in tubes but was very chirpy and did not seem at all phased by the replacement. In fact he was very positive saying that it was actually better as far less was likely to go wrong.

He started his rehabilitation straight away and was very soon up and dressed pacing round the ward. Three weeks later he was Morris dancing!

When Andrew returned from hospital he phoned the wife of the healer to let her know that the operation was successful but then laughed and said that her husband would know that as he was there throughout overseeing it and guiding the surgeon. She laughed too.

Getting fed up with the expense of these appointments, and the time and money travelling to them, I decided enough was enough and we stopped going.

My next trip was to a local Kinesiologist who claimed he could help me. He balanced food on my tongue and muscles whilst lifting my limbs in the air. The idea behind it was to get the body to respond physically to various foodstuffs that I may be allergic to and may therefore be harming my body. He made outrageous statements to check that my muscle responses were correct. He asked if I was a man wearing purple cowboy boots! He said that once he had ascertained how my body was responding with yes and no questions he could find anything out. I kind of understood this theory as I had, many years ago, attended a dowsing course. We would hold a crystal on a chain and ask it to move to yes and no. Amazingly I found the crystal moving in different ways for yes and no; for yes it would swing from side-to-side and for no it would rotate in circles. Even though I was familiar with this concept I honestly expected Jeremy Beadle to walk through the door with a camera crew shouting "YOU'VE BEEN FRAMED"!

He was a lovely man but admitted after a few weeks that he was completely baffled by me and was getting nowhere and would not be charging me for that final session. I admired and respected him for his honesty and not taking my money. He then recommended me to a friend who was a local chiropractor who, he claimed, was better trained than him so an appointment was made to see him.

The chiropractor was really expensive with a swish clinic. After a few sessions he said that all my problems originated from me having buck teeth and a misaligned jaw, which in turn was affecting the whole of my posture and creating a load more problems. He told me I needed to have my jaw broken and set back in place along with braces on my teeth. He said my Doctor could refer me to get a consultation with the hospital and they would arrange surgery.

When I went to the doctor he reluctantly referred me to the hospital. They said it was a load of rubbish and having my jaw broken would actually make my condition worse. On speaking to my dentist he repeated what the hospital had said and although he had heard this theory many times before he had yet to see any positive results. The only option I had was to abandon this theory and having my jaw broken was really not something I wanted done at this time as I was suffering enough pain as it was.

It was becoming completely bewildering and stunning to me to hear how many theories there were on how I had become ill.

So many opinions!!

Also around this time there was a local lady who approached me, telling me she was a healer and for £60 she could definitely "cure" me. Being ever-hopeful I agreed to this and we arranged a time for her to come to my house. When she came, she asked me to lay on the sofa and close my eyes. I must admit to opening my eyes a few times as she chanted and waved her arms frantically over me. This went on for well over an hour, by which time I was falling asleep. She gently touched my shoulder and told me to come back into the room and she would explain what she had done.

She told me that it had been the most difficult healing and she had had to pull me up from the murky mud out of my coffin. She then went on to say that without her I would have definitely died very soon. She told me she had taken me to the aliens and they could not cure me so she had taken me to the angels and they too said they couldn't help me. Having "dragged me back from death" she said that she was sure her own healing powers would have helped and if I would like her to help more, she was happy to come back.

She had arrived with her young son who Andrew had been entertaining whilst this healing occurred. They stayed for tea and cake when her son, aged around 8, announced to me that I needed to get myself better as it was all my own fault that I was ill. On asking him how he had come to that conclusion he said his mummy had told him so. Needless to say I didn't have her back or give her any more money and there was no forthcoming cure. In fact, I felt even worse and out of pocket too!

I was also told — or had read — about the amazing results of molasses, turmeric, ginger, wheatgrass, kelp, glucosamine, super-greens, Omega 3 oil, Noni juice, flax seed, MSM, vitamin C, vitamin D, bee-sting tablets and many more things that I have since forgotten. I tried all of these at great cost for many years, making up revolting concoctions, many of which made me gag, still to no avail. I worked out that I had paid many thousands of pounds on various supplements some of which helped more than others but none were the cure that I hoped for.

Chapter 8 - A Hand-fasting, A Wedding and A Party

A Handfasting

My dear friend Laura rang me one morning, very excited, saying that she and her boyfriend Andy were going to get married.

They were having a hand-fasting in their garden and the neighbours were going to take down their fence and open up the garden so they could have enough room to invite all their many friends and family. She said that she would have liked to have had me as a bridesmaid but appreciated how ill I was but still desperately wanted me there. She told me her neighbour had an all-singing, all-dancing mobility scooter which worked on all terrain and had very kindly offered to lend it to me on the day in the hope that it would encourage me to come. He said he would bring it straight to the car when we arrived so I didn't have to do any walking and when I was leaving he would escort me out and take it back inside.

Although I knew this was going to be extremely difficult for me, I knew how much it meant to her for me to be there. I so wanted to be part of their celebrations. Having known Laura before I met Andy, I had seen her go from being desperately unhappy to ecstatically happy and in love when she met him and I so wanted to be part of their celebrations. She had met Andy through music and they had become partners; singing and playing as a duet. They were a handsome couple and I could see their relationship was going to blossom into so much more. Andy also did music therapy with special-needs people and Laura had two Down's Syndrome children who loved him instantly. Nici, her girl, was a very shy timid girl who wasn't easily drawn in by people but she took an instant liking to him and they formed a very special loving relationship. It was beautiful watching them all fall in love with each other and becoming a loving family. Andy took those children on as if they were his own.

I had been there on all their important anniversaries and helped them move into their beautiful home together. Andrew and I had spent most Christmases with them and Thanksgivings (she is American) too and we always enjoyed being with them all. Laura was an amazing hostess producing feasts for us all to enjoy and Andy was right by her side helping and being a wonderful host. It would have seemed wrong not to be at their wedding. I told her I would try my best to get there.

They asked if everyone, instead of bringing gifts could bring contributions of food and drink as they would struggle with the cost and did not want to compromise on the guest list.

In the meantime Andrew and I went to visit his parents in Leicester and his mum, Lilian, suggested we get a wheelchair and go into Ashby-de-la-Zouch as it was a lovely town to find an outfit for Laura's handfasting. This town was great with its many boutiques and I actually ended up purchasing three incredible skirts. I paid for the one for Laura's hand-fasting, Andrew bought me one and Lilian bought me the third. I think they felt sorry for me that day and sad to see me in a wheelchair. That particular day I was happy to have the sympathy!

Andrew's dad had a Bookers card and we often made use of it while we were staying there to stock up on the staples we used a lot of. We asked if we could all make a trip there to get a big crate of beer for Laura and Andy's hand-fasting. This was agreed.

The day arrived and I was in excruciating pain and wondered how on earth I was going to get there, let alone be sociable. Andrew helped me get washed and dressed and I managed to put some make-up on. Laura had requested an "earthy" dress code and my skirt was a green fairy-type skirt which I loved and I had a lovely little black lacy vest and matching shrug. Andrew collected some ivy from the garden from which we fashioned a headband and I draped some across my shoulders. Andrew got dressed up and we were set to go.

On leaving the house I doubled up on my painkillers and anti-inflammatories. It took nearly an hour to get from my bedroom to the car; every step even more excruciatingly painful than the last. On getting into the car I slumped down in the seat absolutely exhausted.

On arriving, true to his word, Jim, their neighbour came out on the scooter. He was all bubbly and excited and very pleased to see us and it took every ounce of my being to smile and look happy. Inside I was dying with the pain and exhaustion. He had been helping with all the preparations and was telling us about everything as Andrew struggled to get me out of the car and on to the scooter. Once I was in it I felt a bit better and it was very comfortable. Thanking Jim for lending it to me I told him how much it meant to me as without it I probably would not have been able to come. He said he was really glad he was able to offer it to me as he knew what close friends me and Laura were. He said he hoped I enjoyed using it and had a lovely afternoon.

The ceremony was held at the bottom of their garden and was truly beautiful. Laura looked an absolute dream in an exquisite red velvet and tapestry medieval-style dress. Andy looked wonderful, like a dashing prince. It was a very pagan ceremony with vows from the heart and I felt very blessed and honoured to be there. Some weddings are so bland and vows reeled off without much meaning but this was not like that at all. It was very moving. We then all drank from a chalice holding mead, raising it to them individually and wishing them a happy life.

A lot of hard work had been put into the day with several music stages set up. Being musicians themselves they had many musician friends who were happy to play for free — including Andrew. There was such a variety of music from harp music to a very loud, full-on Irish band. Laura had a vision for it to be a bit like a Joules Holland set up and it worked really well. She thought it would make everyone mingle more with entertainment being in different areas.

She was quite right. There were many of my friends there and I found myself quite enjoying the mobility of being able to flit around on the scooter, talking to different people. This concept had become quite alien to me in recent years. The extra painkillers and anti-inflammatories definitely helped and I genuinely enjoyed a large part of the afternoon.

When I could feel the painkillers wearing off I said to Andrew I thought we should go. Laura came over and told me how much she had appreciated me being there and she knew the amount of strength and determination it had taken. I assured her it was all worth it and I would not have missed it for the world. Although I was sad to be leaving early I was over the moon that I had come. Despite them not wanting gifts, alongside the crate of beer we had brought, we presented them with a beautiful Green Man plaque that-

Andrew had bought at a local craft fair. They loved it and it still has pride of place above their fireplace.

Before leaving I went into the neighbours house to go the toilet and as I was getting off the scooter I bumped into a friend who was also needing the toilet. She was horrified at the effort it took me and the pain I was in. She took my arm and tried to help me and I said to her that I didn't know how much more pain I could endure. She rang Andrew later saying she was really worried about me.

Jim miraculously appeared and saw me out on the scooter and said how good it had been to watch me getting around on it talking to lots of people. He agreed with us that it had all gone really well and had been a truly beautiful and special day. Andrew helped me into the car and I thanked Jim and said goodbye.

On returning home, getting back into the house, upstairs, undressed and into bed was one of the hardest marathons I have ever done but over the next few days, lying in bed, I smiled at all the beautiful moments of that day. In fact I still smile when I think of it. It always amazes me how bring-and-share parties always work and there is always the right balance of savoury and sweet dishes. It is one of those things that is simply magic! The feast that was laid on befitted the occasion perfectly.

A Wedding

Jessie and I had been friends since we were teenagers. We had met when I was at college and all we really thought about was where the next party was! Those days were so carefree without much worry about anything. In those early days we had so much fun together going to festivals, parties and concerts together and dancing the night away until the early hours of the morning. Through the years we had drifted in and out of each others lives often just meeting up for maybe a concert or a band from our past, or just a cuppa at each others houses or maybe a walk. We were the kind of friends who would go long periods of time without seeing each other but then just pick up and act like it was just yesterday. I never ever felt uncomfortable with her or lost for words. She was so easy and enjoyable to be with.

She was one of those very special people who was loud and bubbly and always appeared happy. She was always laughing and always lifted my spirits and those of everyone around her. She was a beautiful soul and I loved her dearly. We seemed to grow together and always had lots to talk about with many shared interests. Through my illness she had rung me many times, brightening my life with her laughter and sunny stories.

She had been with her partner, Dean, for some years but despite his many proposals had always said she did not want to marry again. Her first marriage to the father of her two children had ended with him dying from a heroin overdose and she was quite damaged from what went on in that relationship.

Dean was on a trip to visit a close friend in New Zealand and Jessie had stayed behind to look after her children. She found herself missing him dreadfully and this made her realise that he was her love and soulmate and she wanted to marry him. She had rung him and told him this and he was quite obviously totally overjoyed. They booked a hotel where the ceremony and reception would take place.

She rang me and asked if I could join her in the hotel the evening before for her hen night. She wanted me to stay with her and help her get dressed for her special day. I said that, as much as I would love to, I really didn't think I would be able to as I was struggling to do anything. This upset her and she said that she would include Andrew and I in the numbers for the ceremony and the reception. She told me I was to feel under no pressure but if there was any way I could get there on the day it really would make her day complete. She also told me that Dean wanted her to wear a wedding dress but she had told him there was no way that was going to happen. She was a jeans-and-leggings kind of woman and had always found dressing up quite foreign to her.

A few weeks later she rang me, bubbling up with excitement, saying she had actually bought a "proper" wedding dress to surprise Dean on the day and it was beautiful. Until then, she told me, she was going to act very underwhelmed to Dean about what she was going to wear so he would be really surprised.

I had a dress in mind to wear if I did manage to go but didn't dwell on it as I thought, at that time, there was no way I would be able to make it. My previous love of clothes was diminishing as I was barely ever out of pajamas and getting dressed was simply too hard.

The day came and the ceremony was in the afternoon. Laying in bed that morning I felt really sorry for myself and very sad that I would not be there to witness my beautiful friend of many years getting married. Andrew and I had discussed going when we woke up and we both agreed I was just too poorly. Andrew came into the bedroom later that morning and much to his surprise I announced that I now wanted to go, even if we just attended the ceremony and then left. I desperately wanted to see my friend get married in her beautiful dress.

Bless Andrew, he got himself dressed up in a suit and helped me into my underwear and dress. The dress was a size 8 and was not the fitted dress it had been a few months before. My weight was falling away, my muscles wasting and my strength diminishing. With Andrew's help I got very slowly downstairs and out to the car by which time I was totally exhausted. My body was just screaming out in the most dreadful pain imaginable. Andrew thought it was madness and asked me if I was sure it was a good idea. He told me that it was OK to change my mind and I could just slowly make my way back in, upstairs and back to bed. This definitely would have been the easiest and kindest thing to do for my poor body but I said I was determined to go.

The journey there was horrendous. Every bump in the road and stop-start movement jolted my body and made me scream out in pain. As with all the journeys we made Andrew tried his hardest to make it as smooth as possible trying to avoid bumps but it really only took the smallest of bumps to hurt me.

We finally arrived at the hotel and I had to spend a while in the car recovering from the journey and psyching myself up to get out of the car and walk. It was a beautiful sunny day and we slowly made our way to where the ceremony was to take place. There were a number of people milling about including a friend from school who I had not seen for about 15 years. I called out to her and she came over and told me she had been at the hen night and seen Jessie's dress and how blown away Dean was going to be by it. She told me it was stunning and really suited her and she was really excited.

Dean arrived and looked lovely but incredibly nervous. He was shaking with nerves and I tried my best to reassure him that it was going to be OK and to enjoy the day as it would be gone in a flash. Dean told me that Jessie was convinced I would not be there and she was going to be so chuffed when she saw me.

We were all ushered into a room and asked to take our seats. Dean, his best man and the registrar were already at the front. We all sat down and gradually everything went quiet. I think the Wedding March started playing and everyone turned round and even before I saw Jessie I knew she looked amazing by everyone's gasps. Her dress was beautiful and she radiated like only brides do. She had a sunflower bouquet which to me totally summed her up. I had, and still do, see her as a bright sunflower, brightening up the world.

In true Jessie fashion she walked down that aisle laughing and talking to everyone around her. Dean was grinning from ear-to-ear and visibly relaxed as soon as he saw her. She arrived next to him and asked loudly if he was all right. Everyone laughed including Dean and the registrar. My friend Jessie really was a one-off and the only person I have ever known where everyone who met her, loved her, even the ones she didn't like!

After the ceremony everyone left to go outside for the photos but I was struggling to even get off the chair. We sat there for a while while I tried wiggling my toes and feet around to get them awake so I could stand up. Andrew slowly helped me up after everyone had gone and with his help I hobbled outside. The photographs were being taken in the grounds, which was too far for me to walk so Andrew and I sat down on chairs outside contemplating whether to stay for the reception or head home. The sound of Jessie's laughter and all the guests laughing could be heard from where we were. The sounds made me feel happy that my beautiful friend was enjoying her special day and I was happy that the sun was shining.

Suddenly I heard Jessie shrieking "ANGIE!", and I turned to see her running towards me. I had thought she had seen me when she was walking down the aisle but she hadn't. She hugged me and told me how well the wedding had gone and it was a shame I had not been able to see it but she was so glad to see me now. On telling her that I had been there she got very emotional and said how happy she was. I told her how stunningly beautiful, radiant and amazingly feminine she looked, which, of course, she did. She said Andrew and I must come and have some food as a feast had been laid on and there was loads I could still eat on my diet. She said she had had me in mind when making her choices, bless her. She led us back inside to the buffet that had been laid out and proudly showed us all of the food. It was, indeed, a feast. We helped ourselves and went and sat down to eat.

Jessie found us as we were finishing our food and insisted Andrew take a photo of me and her as I was not in the official photos. I think she sensed at that point that we would soon be leaving. Andrew took that photo and although I looked pretty awful in it, I treasure it and the memory it evokes. As we were leaving she came over to us and gave us some cake to take home. She was such a sweetie thinking of me and looking after me on her wedding day.

Unbelievably, 18 months later, I would be attending Jessie's funeral. That day was one of the saddest days of my whole life and I still struggle with the thought that someone who was so incredibly alive and full of all the joys of living can have been taken away from us all. She was one of the most special, amazing people I have ever met and I am honoured that she thought of me as one of her best friends. She is, and always will be, forever in my thoughts. She, like me, loved the summer, warmth and flowers so I am re-minded of her in many moments of my life and can often be found smiling at memories spent with her. Love always my Dear friend wherever you are. xx

A Party

Each year the Morris Men would choose a new area, hire a minibus, and arrange a tour of the local pubs. They would hire a local youth hostel and take the place over for a weekend. They all had their different roles and for a bunch of men it was very impressive how organised it all was right down to one of them making copious amounts of bacon sandwiches for the journey. One of them brought all the food to make enormous fry-ups, which Andrew informed me were the best ever. There was the driver, the bringer of the sticks, a first aider etc. etc.

Andrew had been a Morris Dancer since he was a teenager, initially to enable him to drink beer under age! This was a huge part of his life that he loved. As he got older he also began to teach it. His fellow Morris Dancers had become firm friends and were always there for each other in times of need. It is the best group of male friends I have ever come across. They were happy to show each other their vulnerabilities and would talk at length on a variety of subjects. They were also fun, musical and loved a few beers! They all lived around the forest and a lot of them were keen gardeners growing their own vegetables and making various preserves and chutneys. Each week they would barter with each other with their produce, seeds and handicrafts. This created a lot of variety in our home. Andrew would come home with anything from a few seeds to a big chunk of venison. I always looked forward with anticipation to what he would come home with each week.

They would always rally round for each other, whether it was helping with a house move, visiting in hospital or just needing a friend to go to the pub for a chat and a beer. The ages ranged from young to old but the camaraderie was very strong amongst them all and it was heart-warming to see this amongst men.

Andrew loved the tours and looked forward to them every year; he talked about them for many months after. It gave them quality time together and precious time out to make the bonds stronger between them all and of course create great memories. In the past I had embraced these weekends too. They gave me an opportunity and the perfect excuse to meet up with old friends and enjoy some quality "girly" time and be pampered. Time out for yourself is always good to refresh and renew.

One of these tours had been arranged and Andrew said he really wanted to go but was worried about leaving me on my own. He thought that maybe he could just leave me with some pre-cooked food and wondered whether maybe a friend could come over and keep me company.

Around this time Lorraine had started her training to be a beautician. As well as going to college she had become a consultant for The Body Shop and was hosting parties at home. It gave her some extra cash and was enabling her to learn more about beauty and makeup as within this role she was doing makeup demonstrations. She was showing people how to apply their makeup using different techniques and giving them lots of good beauty tips along the way. She could use the products to give mini-manicures and pedicures, which she said always helped sell them too. This was giving her an opportunity to hone many of the skills she would need when she was qualified. Her dream was to have her own salon so it was also building her confidence and giving her an idea of self employed life.

She was an absolute natural in this role and loved a party so found herself earning quite well and having a really good time. She now had a really good social life and loved that she was being paid to go to parties. She said I should host one as they were a lot of fun, she would do all the work and it would be a really nice opportunity for me to see some of my friends again without having to go out of the house. All that was required of me was to provide some nibbles and drinks for my guests. She went on to say that I would get really good discounts on products, some free gifts and a choice of treatment in the form of a demonstration at the party. The more money that was made the more I would get.

At first this did not appeal to me as getting dressed was too much of an effort and I really did not feel like being sociable. When Andrew mentioned his tour I thought that this was the perfect time to take Lorraine up on her offer. She was over the moon and said she would do everything she could to help and she thought it would be great to invite all my friends. I was to invite as many people as I could as the percentage that actually came was always a lot smaller.

Andrew was pleased that I had arranged something and he could now go away not having to worry about me. Many of the people I had sent invitations to replied saying they would love to come and it would be wonderful to see me. I invited old friends, new friends and a few neighbours.

My friend Laura said she couldn't make it but would love to order some things and asked me to send her a catalogue, which I did. She bought lots of gifts for Christmas and spent over £100. Lorraine was really impressed as at this point she hadn't even done anything!

The weekend arrived and Andrew left on the Friday leaving me food for the next two days. The party had been booked for Sunday and people were to arrive in the early afternoon. Andrew had sorted the dining room out for the party with chairs all around the edge and the table, as Lorraine had requested, at one end of the room.

Lorraine arrived early and sorted out the nibbles and drinks and brought everything she needed for her demonstrations and samples of the products. She set up an oil burner too so that the room would smell nice and encourage people to buy the burners and oils. She was surprised to see all the chairs and asked how many people were coming. When I told her that twenty five people had accepted my invitation she was really pleased and said that hopefully she and I would do really well out of it.

My friend Jessie was the first one to arrive and it was so lovely to see her. She was the life and soul of the whole party keeping people amused with her funny stories. She also worked hard through the afternoon and early evening running up and down the stairs making people cups of tea and coffee.

All my dear friends arrived and were so pleased to see me expecting absolutely nothing from me. The afternoon was fun and very sociable and it was nice to see my old friends interacting with my new ones and the whole ambience was wonderfully joyous. Catching up with my friends was a real tonic and I managed to talk to them all and find out what was going on in their lives. It made me feel a bit bad about the apathy I had had towards the idea when Lorraine had first mentioned it to me.

Lorraine worked really hard doing demonstrations and pampering the ladies with massages manicures and pedicures. She also did a raffle to win a big basket of wonderful pampering treats. She is a great saleswoman as well as a hard worker so by the end of the day it was obvious that with all the orders we must have made quite a lot of money.

The last person to leave was Jessie as she had stayed behind to help tidy up and do the washing up. That was so like her to be thinking of me and wanting to help. She flew around my house that day like a little fairy and as always everyone loved her. Amazingly she only, at that point, had a few months to live!

Eventually Lorraine and I could sit down and talk about the day and count up the orders. Lorraine said that it was the longest party she had ever done and she was exhausted and suggested we order a takeaway. I phoned our local Indian restaurant, which was just up the road, and ordered some food.

After we had eaten and were both feeling a bit better Lorraine said she wanted to add up the orders and work out what I was owed. We had taken £700, which Lorraine said was the most she had ever taken. This enabled me to treat myself to a lot of gorgeous treats, which was a bonus to a wonderful day of seeing all my beautiful friends. Although I was tired and in pain I felt very content. Lorraine then said that we needed to draw the winning raffle ticket as she had forgotten to do it. This is not very ethical but she said I could either draw it randomly or just choose who I wanted to have the beautiful basket of goods. Jessie had worked so hard serving everyone so I said I would like her to have it. If she had known I had done that she would never have accepted and I guess this is the point where I need to apologise to my friends for the dishonest raffle that day!! SORRY xx

Lorraine made sure I was ready for bed and comfortable before she left and I went off to bed and she returned home. Andrew was due home the next day.

Andrew got home full of stories of his weekend. He was really pleased to find that everything had been tidied away and that there was nothing he needed to do. My friends really are the best and I love them all. It was nice to be able to share stories of my weekend too and we were both better for it.

When I rang Jessie to tell her she had won the raffle she shrieked down the phone practically deafening me. She was over the moon and said that when her order arrived she would come and collect them both together. She said it was so good to see me and she would love to come again so we could share some more time together. She had adored our house and garden and the views of the forest.

When her order came I rang her. She said she was off work as she had a cough she wasn't shifting and felt under the weather with flu-like symptoms. She said she didn't want to pass anything on to me so would wait to come over until she was better.

Several weeks went past and I had not heard from her so rang her house. Her daughter answered and said her mum was at the doctors as she still had the cough and it was getting worse. That evening I asked Andrew if he minded driving to her house as the basket would no doubt cheer her up and she could pamper herself with all the goodies, which would hopefully speed up her recovery. He said he was happy to do that and drove to her house the next day.

Her daughter answered the door and was delighted to see Andrew at the door with the gorgeous basket. She said her mum was in bed but she would be really happy to receive it and thanked him for driving all that way.

Chapter 9 - Yoga From a Chair

Andrew said we should take my car up to the forest and see if I could drive in one of the car parks. There are a number of car parks up there which are always empty so this seemed the most logical place to go.

Besides that it is very beautiful up there. I loved living and working around the forest and never tired of its beauty. Most people that live there seem to stay and I met a lot of people that had lived there, moved away, and found themselves drawn back. One of these people was Andrew himself. The forest is captivating and very magnetic. Its magic drew me in and I loved it. Although it is no longer my home I still find myself drawn back there from time to time and as soon as I enter it there is a very strong feeling of coming home. Being a bit of a nomad and having been blessed to live in many beautiful places I have this feeling with several areas. The area that sticks out in my mind and draws me back like a magnet is The Long Mynd; a heath and moorland plateau that forms part of The Shropshire Hills. It is outstandingly beautiful and never fails to take my breath away. It is the nearest I have found to fairy land in England.

Andrew drove to one of the car parks in the forest and I got into the driving seat. It was not a good start as I could not even turn the key to start the car. My fingers and wrists were too swollen, weak and painful to be able to make that move. It is quite soul-destroying when things I had never even thought about doing I was now finding impossible. Andrew, however, was not going to let me give up that easily so he turned the key and started the car. The driving itself went pretty smoothly although I struggled with the handbrake. After a while he drove the car home. Andrew decided he was going to make me a gadget that would make turning the key easier and after a few attempts he actually managed this. He had fashioned a long handle made of wood, filing out a groove that fitted the shape of the top of the key. I could put the key into this, place the handle on top and hey presto I could turn it! Andrew is a master craftsman and very clever at working out problems and creating great master pieces of art. Even this handle was a piece of art and so ingenious. I was one step nearer to driving!

Following that day we made regular trips to the forest car park where I found myself building up confidence again. I learnt that the handbrake was still OK at the level that was comfortable for me to set it at. Amazingly my feet were fine on the pedals and I could actually change gears. The time came to go out on my own.

In our village magazine I had seen yoga for the disabled advertised. This would be carried out sitting in a chair. On reading this I wondered if I could manage it. It was to be a 6 week course on a Tuesday afternoon in a town about 10 miles away. After talking to the facilitator of the course on the phone I booked and paid for it and made the brave decision to drive there on my own.

The day came and with Andrew's help I got outside and into my car. With my amazing new wooden handle I turned the key and was set to go. Andrew waved me off and I drove off up the road. I felt a mixture of feelings as I drove off on my own towards the town. There was a part of me that screamed "woohoo I am doing this". The feeling of freedom and joy of doing something independently was there and these feelings were great to be experiencing. But the other part of me was very nervous. The act of driving comes with many responsibilities and these felt very heightened on that journey. I found myself wondering if this was a good idea and questioning whether my responses would be quick enough if something or somebody was to appear in front of me that would make me have to do an emergency stop. I drove slowly and as safely as I could. The feeling I had reminded me of the time after I had passed my driving test many years before — nervous and exhilarated all at the same time and very alive!

Pulling into the car park it was a relief to see a good parking space next to the hall and it was empty. I parked up and got out of my car and hobbled into the hall.

The first person I saw on arriving was an elderly disabled person who I had once cleaned and cared for. The local church had approached me and asked if I could help her as she was not coping. They said they couldn't pay me but could reimburse my travel so I agreed to do a month at her house and would try my best to get her house back into shape. She had a big, rambling three-storey house which I had cleaned in next to no time, running up and down the stairs and whizzing around. I would stay on after cleaning and get her lunch together and we would sit and chat. She was an interesting lady and an artist. She had many paintings scattered about and was pleased when I admired them.

She had often commented on how fit I was and she wished she was as young and fit as me. Finding myself next to her now in this hall it was a shock to see that I was now a lot more disabled than her. She didn't show any signs of recognition, which I was relieved about as I felt incredibly awkward and embarrassed. The average age was probably about 80 and I was less than half this age, which made me feel even more uncomfortable. All these elderly people looked fitter and more mobile than I was. The exercises were all carried out sitting down and there were many I could not do as a lot of my joints were stiff or damaged. I know it should not have mattered but I felt inadequate that these oldies were in better shape than me and managing to do much more than I was capable of doing and after 3 sessions I called it a day.

Luckily I have grown a lot since then and embrace whatever situation I am in and just do what I can to the best of my abilities. After all that is all any of us can do. In fact I have got so good in these situations that I even embrace being the worst at something as it enables other people to feel better! Generally there are always going to be people who are better than you and life really is not a competition. Enjoy being in the moment and don't worry what other people are thinking. They are probably having all the same worries and insecurities as you.

At least on my way home I felt proud to be driving. Incredibly on this outing I got caught on a speed camera doing 34mph in a 30 limit! My renewed driving was very short and sweet as the pain in my body became too acute to allow me to safely drive.

Chapter 10 - Friends

Gradually friends would hear that I wasn't very well. I had a very good friend, Ken, who I had known all my adult life and we had done loads of adventurous outdoor things together as well as having had a business making shoes and boots.

He was very into self-survival and we had done courses together and cooked and camped in the wild. We had also done lots of wild swimming together in lakes, rivers and the sea. He was one of my longest and most loyal and dearest of friends and I really thought our friendship would survive anything and was pretty much unconditional. We had become, over the years, very close and had shared a lot of personal things together.

I had told him, on the phone, several times how ill I was but he never responded like I would have expected him to. One day he phoned the landline, which was downstairs, so obviously Andrew answered it as I now spent my entire life in bed upstairs. Andrew was trying to do a million things and was very flustered and abruptly told Ken that I was stuck upstairs and he had to go as he was busy. He told me about this call and said he felt he had been a bit rude but was so flustered at the time.

Later Ken rang me on my mobile, very confused saying that Andrew had implied I was really ill and what was going on? I said I had been trying to tell him that myself on several occasions. He said he assumed I just had flu or something. He was used to me always being well and had not taken what I was saying on board as he just assumed I would bounce back. He then went on to say that he must come and "look at me".

He arrived a few days later with a workmate I did not know and only stayed a very short time. I had got myself up and dressed and into the dining room but he was quite clearly shocked to see that my movement in all my joints was very stiff and I was no longer that wild, vibrant friend he had had. He spent the whole visit trying to convince his mate how fit I had been. In the few years that followed I saw very little of him and I must admit that this hurt. I now understand that he was really struggling with coming to terms with me being so ill. He also was going through a lot of hard changes in his own life at the time.

Other friends would come over and when they saw me would start crying and I would end up having to counsel them!

There were a few friends that I would phone and cry on when I was struggling but I soon realised that they were getting fed up with it and my time of them sympathising was coming to an end. It became obvious that if I was to keep my friends I had to somehow come to terms with my life as it now was.

Often I would phone Laura, as I always had, and I guess I had got into a habit of moaning about my pain and how I was struggling to cope with it. She told me that it sounded awful but she now dreaded my phone calls and when the phone rang she found herself hoping it wasn't me. She had a lot on her plate with her children and I realised that it really wasn't fair to be burdening her with my problems. I am grateful for her honesty that day and it was a wake-up call that somehow or another I had to accept my life as it was and go within and work out ways to calm my mind.

My ex-sister-in-law, and dear friend, Karen, was very good at being there for me as a friend and adviser. She was always at the end of the phone if I needed a chat and always listened to me with sympathy. Having done so many things with her over the years, including climbing Ben Nevis, I am sure she must have struggled to come to terms with the state I was now in. If she did she never voiced it but just stayed strong and there for me.

She came to my house quite a few times, bringing with her yummy healthy food for us to enjoy together. She would lie in bed with me and we would talk and laugh together about all the old times and she would bring me all the gossip. These times were precious to me as I found the continuity of our long friendship very comforting and we were basically the same with each other. There was not the awkwardness with her I was finding with other friends who were struggling with what to say and how to act. We went back a long way and had known each other from school days. We were at college together and ended up marrying brothers .... and then divorcing them! We had been a part of each others lives for a very long time and knew each other really well, warts 'n' all! Incredibly, after I met Andrew she started to go out with the man that worked for him (she had known him as a friend for many years before that) and they ended up getting married. Our lives just continued to be intertwined.

When she came to my house she would do a Reiki on me before she left, leaving me to sleep peacefully. She has always been a very special friend to me and still is. There are many qualities of her I admire and love. She is a sister to me and I love sharing our journey through life together.

Andrew sang and played with many fine musicians and he had run an amazing open mic session with a Steiner friend of his. I met and made many friends there including a beautiful lady called Liehsja, who played the harp. She was not only a great musician but had studied and was very intrigued with the health benefits of music, particularly on the heart. She approached me and asked if I minded her coming each week to play her harp in my bedroom. To her it would be her practice and hopefully I would enjoy it and benefit from it. I jumped at this opportunity and told her that it would be lovely. She said she appreciated how ill I was and there was absolutely no pressure to communicate with her. I would be free to sleep, cry, laugh or react in whatever way I wanted to. She would come, set up her harp, play and simply leave with no expectations from me at all.

She was true to her word and it was like having an angel appear in my bedroom each week, playing the most divine and soothing music. Sometimes it was sociable and we would talk, laugh, and eat and other times she would simply play and go. This to me was a true gift and blessing and definitely healed me on many levels. How many people can say they have had that? The people that were coming into my life were truly amazing, especially as I was not even going out and socialising. On a few occasions she even let me play her harp. This instrument has such a lovely sound that even when you can't play it, it still sounds beautiful. To me the harp is a heavenly, healing instrument and without a doubt my favourite of all the instruments there are.

My friend Mandy came round to see me. She had, once upon a time, been my party buddy. We would go out and get drunk and dance a lot. She was upset that I was no longer that person and thought I should take the conventional drugs. She said I should stop taking stupid herbs and watching charts of blood tests. I knew that even if I fully recovered, by whatever means, I would never be that friend she wanted again. I had far more respect for my body now. In fact I am now completely teetotal and very happy to be that way. When I got a wheelchair she came over a few times to take me out shopping and we did have a lot of fun together. We acted out scenes from Little Britain and she would pretend to be angry and abandon me in the middle of shops. It was nice to be out messing around again. We had always had a lot of fun together and also done quite a bit of travelling together around the country.

Lots of people rang Andrew saying how sorry they were to hear how ill I was. Many said "if there is anything I can do, let me know." I grew to hate, and still do hate that expression. My good friend Lorraine would just turn up and look around and say "Where's the Hoover?", "Where's the washing?" and she would just get on with things that needed doing. That to me is true friendship and proper help.

If people are in dire need, do something practical rather than that rather empty statement above. I personally think that this statement can be just a way of people opting out with a clear conscience!

Think what can be done and do it!

Recently a friend was telling me that she had been told a friend of hers had been diagnosed with cancer and had a very short time to live. My friend said she didn't know what to do, she wanted to send her a card but didn't know what to say so she thought she was just going to do nothing. She is particularly good at choosing lovely cards and I have had many such cards from her. I told her to go out and choose a card she knew her friend would like and just simply write inside that she was thinking of her with lots of love. Who wouldn't want to receive that.

While I was ill people sent me lots of cards and every single one of them I appreciated. Looking at a card on my bedside table from a friend with a nice picture and a few nice words made me feel special and loved. Knowing that people were thinking of me always cheered me up as my life had become very lonely and insular. It really isn't rocket science that the smallest of gestures can mean the world to someone. My friend was so grateful to me that I had made what she thought was such a hard task very simple and she said that is what she was going to do. I have no doubt that she would have picked the perfect card and it will have lifted her friends spirits.

It is weird that people I thought I would always be able to rely on were no longer around but incredibly, new people were appearing in my life. One of these people was a new neighbour of ours, Maddy.

She and her husband had moved in and I would watch her sometimes out in the garden, attacking the brambles and overgrown hedges, creating a lovely garden space. She reminded me a bit of my former, enthusiastic fit self. Andrew had spoken to them several times over the wall and they had enquired about me.

They said that we should all get together one day and have a barbecue. Maddy was quite pregnant by this time and to be honest I had no interest in meeting and socialising with them. By this time I was continuously in my pyjamas and often not that clean either as washing had become very difficult. The last thing I wanted to do was meet new people!

Andrew told Maddy but she was not taking no for an answer. So they both agreed a date for a barbecue in our garden. However, this did not happen as she was rushed to hospital with a premature labour. A few weeks later I was on my way out to a hospital appointment and she appeared with the baby in a carrycot. She literally dumped her over the wall. The baby, Holly, was a beautiful little girl and Maddy, as Andrew had said, was really lovely. She told me she was a hairdresser and if I needed my hair doing she could come round. I said that would be good as I had not been able to get to a hairdresser for a very long time.

She came round and tidied up my hair for me and we quickly became firm friends. She was so compassionate and caring and I adored her baby girl. Holly would sit in our washing basket happily playing with the pegs for hours while we chatted. After a few years of my very strict diet Maddy felt very sorry for me and would occasionally smuggle in large bars of chocolate which I have to admit to eating! It was lovely having her as neighbour and she often popped by and cheered me up. We have remained friends even though we now live a long distance away from each other.

It was very awkward for me to phone people and tell them of my illness. How do you ring someone and say, "Oh, by the way, I'm a cripple"? At what point do you fit that in? So I just didn't bother. To this day some people I have been friends with probably still do not have a clue about what I've been through and likewise I do not know what is happening in their lives either.

There was also a few people, especially men, who asked to come and see me and I just could not bear for them to see me in the state I was in. These were friends I had always met when I was out, dressed up and looking good. For them to see me now looking so drab was just too much for me. I am sure they wouldn't have cared but my stupid vanity and pride kicked in.

This meant that gradually a lot of people just disappeared from my life, some to return and some not.

One day a magazine was sent to me called Cygnus review. I started reading it and very nearly dismissed it as religious twaddle, when something caught my eye about angels. This had become a subject I was interested in since my angelic experience.

It turned out to be a book club for spiritual reading. This was exactly what I needed and I ordered 10 books as not only were they cheap, you got a further discount on the first order. On talking to my friend Karen a few days later I mentioned it to her and said what great synchronicity it was and a great gift as this is exactly what I needed. She admitted she was a subscriber and had ordered it for me, bless her.

This turned out to be a real lifeline and I read about meditation, angels, and nutrition, along with many other self-help books. This monthly magazine had spiritual leaders writing their own stories and poems and book reviews. I went on to order many more books on a variety of subjects, which not only helped pass the time but taught me a lot about being positive and helping myself.

As I laid in bed even holding a book and turning the pages was really hard but I still managed to devour book after book. Andrew and I had never had a television but one day Alistair, my Bowen therapist, suggested to Andrew that we should get one. He felt that my life was too insular and I didn't have enough stimulation. Andrew took this on board and went out and bought a TV with a built-in DVD player and we proceeded to buy and borrow as much comedy as we could find.

My opinion is that laughter and comedy are both an essential part of anyone's life but even more so if you are lonely, old or sick.

It was amazing to hear my laugh again and created a much lighter atmosphere in our house. I had almost forgotten what my real laugh sounded like and I realised how much I had missed my own laugh. My life had become heavy with pain and there had not been much real laughter in our house for a long time. Laughter had always come very easily and naturally to me and it was great to have it back.

Andrew still went out a lot, which I think he needed to keep his sanity. He worked from home and looked after me and had to do everything as I was now incapable. He needed time out. His whole business was based around music and he did many gigs and he was also a Morris dancer.

Although Andrew was loving and patient and I was incredibly well looked after with him cooking yummy organic meals for me I do remember that time as being very lonely. Most of my time was spent on my own — in bed. Generally I only really saw Andrew at meal times. There is no blame there as he simply had so much on his plate. He would sometimes play his concertina or mandola and sing to me, which was lovely.

He was playing a lot of music with a lady friend and they were getting a lot of gigs as a duet. As well as the gigs Andrew would go to her house one evening a week to practice. She had become my friend too and I got on well with her.

One day Laura rang me and said she was aware of all the time Andrew was spending with this lady and she was worried for our relationship. I told her that I trusted both of them implicitly. Andrew is the last person to have an affair I told her. She said that that is how Andy and her had got together and there is a big connection formed when you play music that only musicians understand.

Thinking on this and now not having a physical relationship with Andrew I started worrying. After all, I was hardly the ideal partner and part of me understood what Laura was saying but Andrew really was the most honest man, full of integrity, that I had ever met and I knew he still loved me.

A few weeks later I did talk to him about it and he seemed quite shocked that I could even think such a thing. Sometimes she would come to our house and it was obvious that she thought the world of me and I stopped worrying although I was quite jealous of their relationship sometimes. It was obvious that Andrew off-loaded on her and they had a lot of precious moments together playing music … I think, ill or not, this is the life of living with a musician and he hadn't actually changed, it was me who was changed. I had to live with that and accept it. I was blessed with a lovely partner and lots of very good friends and I was actually very grateful.

One day Andrew came home from his evening out Morris dancing and one of the Morris dancers wives had given him a book for me to read to hopefully cheer me up. This book was called Around Ireland With a Fridge by Tony Hawks. It certainly did cheer me up, it was hysterical. I started reading it and it was so funny I started laughing hysterically and loudly.

Andrew heard me from his workshop and ran upstairs to see me. He was seriously worried about me, not re-alising that I was reading and thought I had finally cracked up and lost the plot. It was a great relief to him that I was still sane and laughing at something that was genuinely funny. This is a book that I would rec-ommend to anyone but be careful where you read it as it really is laugh-out-loud humour.

One of my best friends, Lorraine, would phone me regularly and one evening she rang to say that she had met a new man at work and they had started dat-ing. She was eager for me to meet him so I suggested they come over for dinner one evening. He was nice and easily accepted my predicament as his mum had suffered from MS for many years. She was quite clearly a very inspiring lady. He told me that doctors had told her that when you have MS there is never any im-provement; you either stay the same or get worse. She had started going to the gym and practising yoga and, despite what the doctors had told her, her health had improved greatly. She had gone on to set up a pro-gramme for other MS sufferers to help them too. He was obviously very proud of his mum and talked about her with great affection and I found myself warming to him. I warmed to him even more when Lorraine told me the next day, on the phone, that he had said she should come and visit me more as I was in great need of her friendship stuck at home.

Lorraine voiced that she was upset with Andrew that he would not get me a wheelchair. He believed that if I got one, I would never have the incentive to walk again and it would be a downward spiral. Lor-raine wanted to take me out but felt without a wheel-chair it was too hard. She was also upset that Andrew was refusing to put up grab-rails in the house as he did not want his home looking like a disabled house.

Lorraine's boyfriend's mum used a wheelchair and was in the process of updating it to a better one. Lorraine asked her if she could have the old one for me. She tentatively brought it round and although Andrew was not overly happy he did, thankfully, accept it with grace. I grew to love this wheelchair as it really opened up my life and Lorraine and a few other friends took me to lots of lovely places. I loved that Lorraine fought for me and helped me to improve my quality of life when I was basically too weak. She was there for me in all my difficult times.

She did many personal things that only a best friend would do. She helped me put my knickers on in hospital and, as my armpits were smelling, she washed them. She has always visited me in my real times of need.

Lorraine and I had been friends for many years before my illness. We had met when we worked together in an accounts office. The company we worked for was within a big mansion set in many acres of beautiful gardens. Although the job itself was not very exciting the company was a good one with many benefits. Lorraine had continued in various accounting jobs but while I was ill she started to train to be a beautician. She asked me if I could be her guinea pig on some of the treatments she was learning. She would come round to my house and give me beautiful manicures and pedicures.

My consultant once commented that I had the prettiest feet out of all her patients and I definitely have Lorraine to thank for that. The best treatment was one where she would cover my hands and feet with hot wax, leave it to harden and then peel it off. It was not only beautifying, making my hands and feet soft, but incredibly therapeutic on my painful, swollen joints. She now has her own salon, *Absolute Beauty*, in Seaford, Sussex, which is a total treat to go into. I still get my toenails cut and beautifully painted and embellished whenever I'm in that area.

Lorraine and I have seen each other through our divorces and many life traumas and although, on the surface we are very different, we are true friends. I am forever grateful for the part this beautiful lady plays in my life.

I have a very dear Australian friend, Bronnie. We met in an office that I worked in many years ago and since then she had returned to Australia. We had regularly written to each other for many years, keeping our lovely friendship alive. Andrew and I had visited her in Australia at the beginning of our relationship and had travelled through Australia with her and met her family. She had shown us some amazing places and we had all enjoyed each others company.

While I was ill I poured my heart out in letters to her telling her of how difficult my life had become and the pain I was now in. I told her I was really trying to stay the positive, happy person I had always been but that it was becoming harder and harder. Bless Bronnie, in her wisdom, she encouraged me to tell her everything and not leave any detail out. She assured me that she didn't mind and genuinely wanted to know what was going on as that was my life at the time. I sent her many letters of woe and appreciate to this day the therapeutic effects this had on me.

She would write back with comfort and sympathy and update me with her life, which was always colourful and a joy to hear about. We had both been there for each other over the years, albeit from a distance, and had managed to keep the friendship strong .

I think we should be proud that we still feel such a strong connection with each other after being friends for over 20 years and probably only actually seen each other for less than 20 weeks in total!

We have always had a telepathy with each other and somehow know when the other is going through some kind of trauma. I love this. There are many things in life that we do not fully understand and I like that. It is the mystery and magic that keep life interesting.

Obviously now with social media and emails it is a lot easier to keep in touch but sometimes I miss getting that wad of paper handwritten, with some photos wrapped in the middle, landing on my doorstep. I am a great believer in writing things down in order to let them go and Bronnie enabled me to do this.

Chapter 11 - Affirmations and Gratitude

Within a lot of the self-help books I read, I began to learn the importance of self-affirmations, mantras and visualisations and believing that things would get better. I learned that affirmations should always be said in the present tense.

Often, when I was lying in bed unable to move I would say things like, "I am well", "I am walking", "I am swimming", "I am amazing". My favourite affirmation then and still is now is, "All is well." I find this very comforting when I am scared and often extend it to, "Everything is as it is meant to be".

As I said these affirmations to myself I said them with as much conviction as I could muster. This conviction would vary from day-to-day depending on how positive I was feeling on any particular day. This became a regular practice and I started actually visualising myself walking, swimming, driving etc. and over time I found myself really believing that all these things would actually be so.

As with any exercise, whether it be physical or mental, over time and regular practice I got better and better at doing this and became happier, more positive and full of hope.

These affirmations, I learned, were a way of rewiring my inner beliefs and by doing this, were becoming more successful.

After some time I began really enjoying these exercises and becoming more and more confident of my recovery.

Along with these exercises I started to think of all the things I was grateful for. At first I found this very difficult but I started with "I am grateful that I have a roof over my head".

As time went on my list of gratitudes got longer and longer and I found myself naturally being more grateful for everything in my life.

There are always so many things to be grateful for. Most of us have heating, running water, a comfortable bed, food on the table, eye sight, hearing, clean sanitation, someone who loves us, family, friends, money, the ability to smile, talk, sing, etc etc. The list is endless.

All of these things we should be grateful for and the more things you find to be grateful for you just find the list just goes on and on. It is now impossible for me to comprehend that there was a time I was struggling to find even just a handful of things to be grateful for. It is a very good and meaningful practice to do and brings many blessings. By making yourself aware of the blessings in your life it not only makes you happier but opens your eyes to the unfortunate people that do not have all these things that are enhancing your life. You naturally become more compassionate and less greedy and more ready to give. By being grateful, I could focus on all the positive things in my life. Focussing on the positives was much more rewarding than focussing on the negatives.

Each day with my affirmations and lists of gratitudes I found myself much happier, more positive and believing in a much happier and successful outcome for my life.

Chapter 12 - Being In a Wheelchair and Disabled

Being in a wheelchair, I think, is something everyone should experience and I believe there are disability awareness courses where the students are taken out in a wheelchair. They learn to experience people's reactions towards them and all the difficulties experienced by wheelchair users.

At the time of getting a wheelchair this was really my only means of getting around as I could only hobble a few yards. I do remember thinking at the time that this was going to be permanent as I was so crippled. I wished it was temporary (which thankfully it did end up being) as even then I recognised it as being a very interesting experience.

If I found myself being pushed towards people coming towards me, more often than not, they would look very awkward, avoid eye contact and get out of the way as quickly as they possibly could. It was as if there was an evil monster in front of them and they were petrified of having to interact.

At first I found this quite hurtful but as in most things I ended up seeing the humour in it. One little girl asked her mummy "Why is that lady in a wheelchair?" Her mum told her that it was rude to ask, in a very angry voice. Being quite shocked at this reply I said it was not rude at all, it was a perfectly normal and good question to ask. I told the little girl that my legs did not work properly and that the wheelchair enabled me to do all the things I liked doing which otherwise I would not be able to do. If parents act in this way, fearful of the unknown, it just passes that fear down to the children — as is the case with ignorance about any minority group. For this reason I deliberately ask questions about things. I interact with all people, admitting my ignorance on a subject. My experience generally is that if you genuinely want to know something, if you ask it with an open mind and heart people will happily open up. In fact a lot of people are waiting for that and embrace being asked about their faith or whatever it is you are broaching. This is a much nicer way to go through life instead of listening to the media who deliberately incite hatred.

I have developed a practice that I do now every time I go out, usually when I get inside the car. I put my hands in a praying position, close my eyes and centre myself with a few mindful breaths. I then ask my angels (this could be God, The Universe, or just simply an intention for yourself) to protect me from any accidents or harm and ask that all my liaisons be good ones. This probably takes less than two minutes but works. Whether it is my angels answering me (I like to think it is) or just simply because I have set an intention to be mindful of how I am with all the people I meet. It works! I always remember to say *thank you* when I return home too. I think that my life being enhanced for these practices may just be because I am following laws of the Universe that are in return rewarding me. Does it matter how it works? Try it for a day, just being mindful and kind, and I BET YOU FIND YOURSELF HAVING A BETTER DAY.

Another thing that regularly happened to me when I was in a wheelchair was that people would ask whoever was pushing the wheelchair what was wrong with me. They would also ask them what I wanted or any other question they needed an answer to. Being me I would always pipe up that I could talk for myself and please, if they wanted to ask me a question they could ask me as there was nothing wrong with my brain.

Navigating a wheelchair, especially in shops, and up and down kerbs was very hard at times. My friends all did a grand job and they benefited as I would become the shopping trolley! Sometimes I was piled high, hardly able to see in front of me.

If you are reading this please remember that anyone in a wheelchair is a human being and often does not need to be talked to through another person or talked down to. People often seemed surprised to find that I had a good sense of humour and a good personality to go with it.

It is strange and very human, I think, that if we have not experienced something ourselves we find the situation very awkward and either try to completely ignore it or over-compensate. The lessons I learned from being in a wheelchair were invaluable and I am grateful for them, as I am for so many other lessons I learned from being disabled.

My friends and family had been urging me for some time to claim for Disability Living Allowance and get a blue badge. The idea of being branded disabled horrified me and I was too proud to advertise it but in the end I started to realise the benefits that would come from it. It was obvious it would make my life easier and that was certainly needed.

My friend Jane said she was happy to help me with the forms; she was familiar with them as she and her daughter Lucy were both registered disabled. She knew how useless I would be as I was always thinking I was better than I actually was. We had learnt this from the forms at the hospital with the faces on. It was a struggle for me to compare myself to a healthy person. After all this was my life and I needed to see it as positively as I could just to keep my sanity. The trouble is that if I had got dressed that to me was a really good day and I thought I was doing really well. The reality is to a normal person that is just something they do to start their day. To me that could be my whole day. So basically I had completely lost sight of what normal was. I was learning that health and pain were relative. If a healthy person could have felt my pain they would have said it was much worse but as it had happened in stages it was something I just had to get used to and adapt to and of course live with.

Jane came round and we sat down together. She said I must answer all the questions as to how I felt on my worst days. She knew that a lot of my days were spent not being able to do much, if anything. Filling out this form took a long time but I am sure it would have taken a lot longer if I had done it on my own without her help. We put it in an envelope for Andrew to take up to the post office and get it sent off and Jane went home.

This left me totally depressed having written down all the things I could not do. It was as if my cells had heard it all and were responding negatively. Believing in the power of affirmations I realised that this is exactly what was happening. This was the opposite of my positive affirmations that made me feel so much better. I was no longer affirming that I was well but that I was very ill. Instead of concentrating on what I could do I had spent the whole day concentrating on what I could not do. No wonder I felt deflated and depressed!

Some time later I received a letter saying that a doctor from the Work and Pensions department would be visiting and assessing me for Disability Living Allowance. The letter stated that if it was awarded to me my money would be back-dated to the date I had initially claimed. This benefit is to help with the costs with being disabled and is not means-tested. A date and time had been arranged.

The doctor arrived and Andrew let him in and escorted him to the bedroom where I was lying on the bed. Andrew left us, trusting him to be a professional and went back downstairs to his workshop to get on with his work.

Having got myself dressed, at a lot of time and effort for his visit, I was a bit put-out when he asked me to strip down to my underwear to examine me. He said he would wait in the hall and to let him know when I was ready. The effort of taking my clothes off after having just put them on was really hard work and took quite some time. I called the doctor in feeling very uncomfortable and vulnerable sitting on the edge of the bed in my underwear.

He came back into the bedroom and asked me to lie down. He roughly lifted my feet in the air and started trying to bend my knees and put my legs in different positions. I screamed out in pain and he seemed very surprised and asked me if he was hurting me. I told him my feet were very painful, there was hardly any movement in my hips and I could not bend my knees so yes he was hurting me A LOT!

Looking at my body anyone could see that my body was not right. I was grossly underweight and all my joints were severely swollen. My knees looked like footballs and my ankles were non existent with the swelling. He then proceeded to do the same with my arms with the same result — me screaming out in pain. By this time I was really upset and started crying.

He asked me to get dressed and he would then ask me to walk the corridor to see how far I could walk. There was no way now that I could get fully dressed so I struggled into my dressing gown. As I hobbled to the bedroom door and outside into the hall he said he could see that I really could not walk very far and to come back to the bed.

Suddenly he changed and said he was sorry he had been heavy-handed but it was necessary as lots of people pretended to have diseases to get benefits. This was pretty unfair as it was obvious to a blind bat that I was suffering and seriously ill. He then went on to say that it was a horrible disease and in his opinion the most painful. He said he felt very sorry for me and would put me forward to be awarded the benefits that I was quite clearly entitled to. He said he was happy to let himself out and left.

On hearing the back door go Andrew came upstairs to see me. He was shocked to find me on the bed in my dressing gown crying. He asked what had happened and he was furious and said he would never have left me on my own with him if he had known what he was going to do.

Thankfully after all of that I was awarded higher rate Mobility Allowance and middle rate Care Allowance. I have talked to numerous people who are on Disability Allowances and I have never met one that has gone through what I went through that day and no one that has even been asked to take their clothes off.

A few years later I was sent a letter saying that a doctor would be coming to my house to review my DLA. I rang the office and said that the last assessment had left me traumatised and in a lot of pain and I was not prepared to go through that again. They accepted this and cancelled the appointment.

Looking back on this I realise that the doctor was completely unprofessional and I really should have put in an official complaint but of course at the time I didn't know what the proper procedure was and probably would not have had the energy anyway. That is another downside of being weak and vulnerable.

Luckily, obtaining a blue disabled badge was much easier. Having been awarded Mobility Allowance automatically entitled me to one. Along with that I also applied for a Radar key for disabled public toilets. Both of these things made my life so much easier and I wondered at the time why it had taken me so long to do this. I think the answer is BLOODY PRIDE!

I really should have listened to my friends! I admit I can be stubborn and bloody-minded at times and it really is not very attractive.

Going to a town or any busy place became so much easier as we could now park in disabled places and on double yellow lines. We began to realise the importance and convenience of Blue Badge parking spaces. This became a subject that Andrew would end up getting angry about.

For us to go out anywhere took a lot of preparation, time and energy, and having a disabled parking place was very important for many reasons. We needed extra space for me to get out of the car as I could only get out if the car door was fully open. Andrew then had to get the wheelchair from the boot and wheel it round to the front so I could be helped directly into the chair. This process could take 30 minutes at worst and it was often very painful and stressful.

At one point, after a stay in hospital, I was sent to the local sports centre for some rehabilitation and more often than not mothers would park in the disabled places. They would either sit and wait for their children to come out or park in a disabled place and go inside to collect them. Andrew had quite a few arguments with these mums. Even when he calmly explained our situation they would say, "I'm only going to be a few minutes"as if that made it acceptable.

Unfortunately, if you have never been a disabled person or a carer it is almost impossible to comprehend how hard everything is for that person. More disability awareness should be taught so that people have a better understanding of, and compassion for, people that are less able than themselves. Their lives are very hard and challenging at times and some consideration and respect should just come naturally.

Sometimes these outings would be the first time in a long time that I had gone out and the last thing I needed, on top of all my problems, was confrontation. Andrew has always said that he too is grateful for the insights of the disabled and carers life as he had never previously been aware of any disability issues at all.

All my friends and family were unfortunately learning of all the complications that now went with my life. My friend Lorraine admitted, when I told her I was going to commit suicide, that she just thought I couldn't walk very well and was very shocked to know of all the other things I could not do. I guess some of this was my own fault as I found it embarrassing to admit to all the things (in fact most things) I could not do.

At my worst the disease had reached my jaw and I could no longer chew properly or even talk properly. I could not feed myself or lift a glass to drink. Personal hygiene I could no longer do for myself and I felt beyond useless. Andrew had the patience of a saint and was always loving and rarely complained even though he was now doing everything for me. He kept cheery and hopeful of my recovery at all times.

Chapter 13 - Let's Do Our Meditation

Yvonne rang me one day and said there are a lot of people talking about an amazing healer called Burgs, who was coming to Forest Row and doing a weekend retreat. She was going with a friend and asked me if I wanted to go with them. She said she could pick me up and so I agreed to go.

It was in a lovely mansion set in beautiful gardens and two large rooms had been allocated to us. On arrival we were given forms to complete asking various questions, including questions about our health. There was a lovely group of people and gradually everyone started to chat and introduce each other.

After a while a man walked in wearing a bright orange Chinese martial arts outfit. He was very handsome, with blond spiky hair. My initial reaction was "Oh here we go, another charlatan." He went to everyone individually, looking at their forms and briefly chatting with them. He came to me and asked me how I thought I got in the state I was in and I said I felt it was the stress and hurt caused by my family.

When he had seen and chatted to everyone, he called us all into the "meditation room", asking us all to remove our footwear. He asked for everyone that was able to sit on the cushions and for those of us that couldn't, to sit on the chairs at the back.

He started the morning with a simple meditation, watching the breath and then did a short discourse on how the body and mind are connected. We then did some Chi Kung exercises, which to my surprise I could actually do some of. He then did a guided meditation where he started chanting too. This was a beautiful sound and resonated all through my body making me feel very peaceful.

It was not long into the morning when I realised that Burgs was someone special and he really did know what he was doing. He was captivating, energising and also very funny and it was obvious that everyone felt the same way. Throughout the weekend we did many meditations. He carried out group healings and we spent time outside following his Chi Kung instructions and then he left us to just move freely as we felt.

Being outside moving after all the meditations felt amazing. My senses were heightened and I could see the smallest of insects and even hear their movements. There was a small pond and a dragonfly appeared. I was mesmerised by the dance it was doing and the whole beauty of this creature. I felt at one with my whole surroundings, aware of everything around me. I was allowing my body to just move as it wanted to like a tree in the breeze. I felt strong like a tree trunk and my arms were swaying with no friction or stiffness. I have no clue whether those moments were a few minutes or half an hour, but they were truly magical and I had a taster of true peace within myself. It was bliss.

Burgs had also asked us to keep what he called Noble Silence. This involved not talking to each other and he told us that we would gain much more from his teachings and meditations that way. We were, however, allowed to ask him questions. In those moments outside I was so grateful for that silence as I became completely oblivious of other people just the sheer beauty of Nature. I was amazed at how much more I could do physically and was able to enjoy a lot more movement.

Burgs spoke to me at the end of the weekend and suggested I attended a weekend of Chi Kung and Metta Meditation in Devon that he was running the following week. He felt that I would benefit from this as I needed to do a lot of forgiveness on my mother. He asked about my present life and I told him I lived with Andrew and he was recovering from open heart surgery. He became very worried at that point, saying he feared that there could be a nasty entity in our house as it was strange that we were both young and had very serious health problems and could he come round and see. I wasn't quite sure what Andrew would make of this but figured that we had done so many weird and wonderful things he would accept it.

There was no need for me to have worried as when Burgs saw Andrew with a concertina he got really excited and asked him how he made them. He asked if he could have a go. Andrew passed it over to him. They are actually quite hard to play and to our astonishment he played a simple tune. He laughed at our astonished faces and said before he was a monk he seriously played the harmonica in a band and the concertina was the same principle. He fell in love with the concertina and I think for a split second he wanted to buy it.

He then commented that Andrew did not look or sound like a man that had recently had heart surgery. He asked him if he could get his dowsing rods out and check his chakras. By then Andrew and he had quite clearly bonded over concertinas and Andrew said yes, he could and was intrigued by how they worked.

I had already seen this in action during the day as he had tested us all before and after a meditation and the results were amazing. Andrew stood still as Burgs came towards him pointing the dowsing rods at each chakra one by one. He was really impressed that the rods spread wide open on every chakra. He said he was clear of any blockages and asked if he did any spiritual practices and was very surprised when he said no.

He asked if he could look round the house although he now thought his original fears didn't stand. We showed him around the whole house and he was very impressed that it was free of clutter and the floors were natural and everything flowed. He said there was nothing sinister there. Andrew and he shook hands and we all said goodbye and he left.

Yvonne was interested in going on the retreat to Devon with me and we asked if anyone else in Forest Row was going. There was a young man, Russell, that helped Burgs and he said he would be travelling with a friend from Sussex and we were welcome to travel with them if we all shared the cost of the petrol. He suggested that we all meet at his house. Yvonne came to our house and Andrew dropped us both off at Russell's house who lived just up the road.

The four of us travelled together and got to know each other on the journey having lots of laughs and several lovely stop-offs on the way. A lot of the place names tickled our sense of humour and we made up stories around them that involved Goblins and Dwarves. It was good company and fun journeying with these lovely men.

We arrived on the Friday evening and I was allocated a room on the ground floor of this great mansion. This room had originally been the old dairy and was very small, basic and very cold, which kind of felt apt in a monastic type of way! There were quite a lot of people I recognised from the Forest Row retreat and we all gathered in the meditation room. Burgs gave us an itinerary of the weekend and an introduction and we then all went to the dining room for supper. The

Noble Silence was enforced here too — so we ate in silence.

After the meal we washed up our stuff and were left to do whatever we wanted before retiring to bed. The next morning was an early start of meditation and Chi Kung. Burgs was determined that everyone started with the right posture and made me go to the front where he physically manipulated me into position. He even adjusted my clothes so they were straight. He said if he could get me in the correct position everyone else would follow. This was quite intimidating but I was desperate to learn from him and by co-operating I did find myself feeling better.

Over the weekend we were taught Metta Meditation and the importance of forgiveness. We meditated, chanted, and did various breathing exercises and even some yoga. The best meditation was, and still is for me, the Metta Meditation where you say to yourself, and really mean it, "May I be happy." Then go out to the people in the room, "May all beings be happy" and further and further out saying, "May all beings be happy", right out to the whole world, "May all beings be happy".

Burgs taught us that all any of us basically want is to be happy and we should wish this for everyone, even the people we do not like.

There is room in the world for everyone to be happy, there is room for us to be away from people we do not like and wish them happy. By wishing people that we do not like to be happy we are on the right road to forgiving them. While I was doing these meditations I started to incorporate visualising my sister as I said, "May all beings be happy". Burgs encouraged us to include anybody that we did not like into these meditations.

Russell had told me before the retreat that Burgs had been a monk in Burma and had reached a higher attainment in Buddhist training than any other Western person had ever reached. After seven years of being in the monastery he was told he had to come back to the West and teach what he had been taught. He is an amazing teacher and I am so glad I met him when I did. Without his teachings I would not have learned these valuable lessons and I am sure I would still be knotted up and pretty screwed up about my past. Learning to forgive my mother and sister was very releasing and healing.

Burgs said he was very impressed with my progress but he could only teach me a small amount over a weekend retreat and he recommended that I go on one of his 10-day retreats, which were a lot more intense and far more beneficial. Yvonne and I decided we both wanted to go and found out there was one in Ireland. I asked Yvonne if she would be able to help me with things I could not do, like putting my socks on. She said she was happy to do this so we went ahead and booked the flight to Cork. The airline said they could take me through the airports in a wheelchair and then we would be able to get a taxi from the airport to the retreat.

At this point I had lovely long, shiny hair which Andrew would brush for me every morning and evening. This was obviously going to prove a problem on the retreat so I asked my neighbour Maddy if she would cut it short. It was very sad getting my hair cut but it did feel strangely releasing too. Russell told me later that monks shave their hair because they believe it holds onto negative energy. It was therefore actually releasing a lot of my past which felt good. It also meant that I could at least manage my hair without asking for any help.

It was quite nerve-wracking leaving Andrew for 10 days and I think he was feeling this too.

We had been told before the retreat that along with the Noble Silence we would also have to hand in our mobile phones. We were to have no communication with relatives, friends, or the outside world until the retreat was over. Andrew had been given the number of the retreat in case of absolute emergency but we were all to be totally silent in every way apart from talking to Burgs himself.

Andrew took us to the airport and dropped us off. There is a phone just inside the airport and, as requested, I used it to call for help. A man came immediately with a wheelchair and we were taken right through the airport to the plane. It was a very small plane so 2 men had to carry the wheelchair with me in it up the steps. That was really scary and it felt as if they were going to drop me.

We got seated and I felt quite excited as it had been a long time since I had been on a plane. I love flying, especially the taking off. I was surprised to discover that Yvonne, who has flown loads, hates taking off. I ended up holding her hand, convincing her that all was well.

We landed in Cork and were given a wheelchair to get me to the taxi point. We agreed a price with the taxi driver and I got in the front and Yvonne in the back. The taxi driver was a lively, talkative Irish man and he proceeded to tell us of all the good music, pubs and venues in the area. He told us what a great time we were going to have. I must admit I had always wanted to go to Ireland for the music and the Craic and was a bit miffed to think we were going on a silent retreat and then coming home!

We told him what we were doing and he was astounded and promised us that if we changed our minds at any time during the week he would come and get us and we could stay with him and his wife. He said they would love to host us and take us out to all the best places. He placed his card in my hand as he said this.

When we arrived we paid the taxi driver but he insisted he didn't want to go until he had met Burgs. As we got out of the taxi, Burgs came out of the house and we waved him over to talk to the taxi driver. The driver got out of the taxi and said he had to shake Burgs' hand. He said that Burgs was an amazing man and that anyone that could keep a room full of women quiet for 10 days deserved a medal! Burgs laughed and we all walked off together as the taxi driver drove off shouting that we had his number if we needed him.

We had arrived a day early and were due to leave a day after the retreat so we were all allowed to talk and relax. We met the lovely Irish lady who had helped us organise all the logistics. We then met the lady who owned the retreat. She and her husband and a few staff lived on the premises and she also, apart from hiring the place out, ran her own meditation/ mindfulness retreats. She told me she loved watching everyone arrive and recognised right from the start all the different personalities. She told me that all these personalities were actually needed for such a retreat and miraculously they never failed to turn up. I did not fully understand this at that point but by the end of the 10 days I did. She told me she knew I would gain a lot from the 10 days ahead of me.

We were shown the layout of the place. The women were mainly in a dormitory above the dining room and the men were to sleep in a different building. Due to my disabilities I had a separate room down-stairs through another front door which also led to the kitchen, toilet and shower room. There was also a massive meditation room which was another separate building.

Burgs always had volunteers at his retreats who helped with the day-to-day running of them. The main volunteer on this retreat was Russell who was to help Burgs with anything and everything from the carrying of things to early morning Chi Kung. It was nice to see Russell again as after travelling the long distance to Devon and back with him recently he now felt like a friend.

The volunteers are there to help with the smooth running of these retreats and do everything in a right and proper way with loving kindness being sent out to everyone at all times. To qualify as a server or volunteer you must have sat at least one ten day retreat. This way you fully understand the strict rules, the Noble Silence, and what the students are going through as they hand over all their possessions and just sit with their vulnerabilities, tears flowing and processing their meditations. It can be a very painful experience. Selfless service is an essential part of Dhamma and it serves as a way of showing gratitude and helping to naturally give out loving kindness.

Another volunteer, Kate, had come all the way from Forest Row to do all the cooking. She had arrived with a mass of kitchen utensils and masses of food she had ordered from Infinity Foods. The food on the retreat was all organic and vegetarian.

Burgs asked the few of us that had arrived early if we fancied a trip out and we all bundled into his car (Burgs and Russell had come on the ferry). We went out to a beautiful pub overlooking the sea and we shared a seafood platter. A few of the men wanted to try some of the renowned Irish Guinness but Burgs said that he would prefer everyone to stay alcohol-free as we would be doing an evening meditation and the two did not mix. One man got one anyway but the rest of us were happy not to be drinking.

We arrived back at the retreat centre to find that a few more people had arrived. I met the gardener who told me that he grew all the vegetables and herbs we would be eating and they were all organic. He would also be baking fresh organic bread rolls for us all every day. He told me that all the people that lived at the retreat had come together very quickly with the same shared vision. Everything was eco-friendly right down to the paint on the walls and the organic cotton bedding that was provided. You could literally feel the love and energy that had gone into creating this wonderful retreat and it felt good to be there. The place and its people were very special.

The building that had been specially built as a meditation hall had a shrine at the front. There was a massive Buddha there and beautiful flowers were brought in from the garden, fresh each day, as an offering. There was a beautiful wooden floor with cushions scattered around and chairs at the back. There was also a lot of incense burning and the whole room felt and smelt divine. It was such an awesome place and so peaceful to be in.

Surrounding the retreat were various cliff-top walks which people were exploring but I could barely get from one room to the next. Everyone was coming back saying what wonderful views there were at the top of the cliffs and talking of all the wild flowers everywhere. I was never to see any of the views or flowers they spoke of.

Burgs overheard Yvonne and I discussing how she would come and put my socks on in the morning and take them off for me in the evening and help me with anything else I needed help with. He was horrified and said that she could not do this for me as we were both undertaking our own silent journeys over the next 10 days and there would be a lot of processing that we would have to do. He said that Yvonne would have to choose whether she took the role of carer or not. He said that if she was to become my carer she would not be able to get involved in all the meditations. He told me that Russell or Kate would help me if I wanted but I was not allowed to involve them in any further discussions.

Yvonne said she really needed to fully attend the retreat and therefore would have to refrain from helping me in any way. At that moment I felt very betrayed by her but of course that was being very selfish. Obviously, with hindsight, I am glad for both of us that she made that decision. Russell and Kate were nearly always on hand as I was next to the kitchen and that was where they generally were.

That evening we all communed in the meditation hall and were given an itinerary of the next 10 days. Every day would start at 5am, being woken up in the dark by a bell. We would head straight for the meditation hall then Chi Kung followed by breakfast. Each day was broken up with various meditations, discourses, healings and meal breaks which were quite long. The food was very nutritious and delicious. Each evening finished with a Metta Meditation before we all retired to bed at 9pm. Burgs told us that the Noble Silence was really important and even if we found ourselves wanting to talk we must refrain and respect everyone else's silence.

As far as I am aware everyone kept to this apart from talking to Burgs to question things and for me to ask for help occasionally. He told us that after the last meditation at the end of the 10 days we would be allowed to talk again. He said that we must wait until we had left the meditation hall as he wanted that to stay silent at all times. I could at that point visualise everyone running outside and talking 19-to-the-dozen about the week and their experiences. He told us that most of our talking was unnecessary burble and the majority of communication was non-verbal. I was amazed as the retreat progressed to find that I felt I knew all the people there and their personalities even though no words were being exchanged. Living together, meditating, eating and observing, tell us far more about people than words. You see whether people are tidy, greedy, selfish, punctual, kind, or clumsy.

There was one woman who questioned everything, Burgs said. She refused to use a cushion and brought her own bean bag instead. Burgs told her this was not suitable but she refused to listen to him and carried on using it in the meditation hall. It was grubby and she fidgeted a lot, creating noise amongst the silence. At one point the bean bag burst and the little beans were dispersed across the immaculate pine boards. It seemed that everyone but her had noticed this. She took food that was labelled specifically for people with special dietary needs and never took a turn washing or wiping up. I think at some point during the retreat everyone was irritated by her, even Burgs himself.

At the Metta Meditations Burgs would ask us to include someone we disliked or who irritated us, whether it be on the retreat or in our personal lives. We were to send that person loving kindness and to wish them happy. At the end of the retreat a lot of us admitted to have aimed it at this woman — she was getting a huge whammy of loving kindness from us all each day.

There was an afternoon towards the end of the 10 days when Burgs offered time out and said that a man had offered to take us out on his boat. On arrival the man said he would not be able to get me on or off his boat and even if he could it would be too dangerous as there were no seats and if it was rough I could get thrown around. He said everyone needed to be sure-footed for the expedition.

This was so disappointing for me as I had been looking forward to the boat trip but I tried graciously to accept that I could not go. Another lady decided she didn't fancy going and we stayed behind together and ended up becoming friends. The owner of the retreat also joined us and we discussed further the phenomenon of knowing people better in silence. She mentioned the bean bag lady and said she knew straight away that she would be the one who irritated us all and asked me if she was right. My part in the retreat, I think, was for people to learn to develop their skills for compassion by trying to understand my situation. There were kind people there, the helpers and many more characters. The owner told me how she marvelled at every retreat that all these people "turned up" and she had become an expert in recognising all of them individually.

Burgs had warned us that at the retreat without outside distractions (no books, TV, phones or any reading matter) with mindful meditation a lot of things would come up and we could find ourselves very emotional. He assured us that he would check on us all individually and help us through all the stages.

A few days into the retreat I found myself very tearful and retreated to my room. I started sobbing uncontrollably and I think Russell heard me and went to find Burgs. Burgs came to my room and asked me what was happening. I told him that I could not stop crying but I didn't know why. He replied that I didn't need to know why but it was really important that I just let it all out. I felt totally bereft and he just left me there sobbing my heart out. This went on solidly for about 24 hours. Burgs came to me periodically and said it was OK and that other people were experiencing the same thing. He told me that when I did stop crying it was up to me whether I continued with the retreat.

After I stopped crying I felt a lot better. The awareness dawned on me that I had never properly grieved for a lot of things, including my loss of mobility and the life I had been used to before that. A feeling of sheer determination hit me and I thought to myself, "Yes, I am going to continue this retreat, bring it on!" and I returned to the meditation hall.

When Burgs had visited me during my crying time I had voiced that I was fed up as everyone was going on wonderful walks, seeing the beautiful cliffs and coastline. All I could do was sit outside on a bench or hobble to my room. He pointed out that I was actually luckier than all the other people as the views and the walks were merely distractions. All I had to do was process my meditations. This is a lesson that has stayed with me.

A few days later, when we were all on one of our long breaks and everyone had wandered off, Burgs came to me. He asked me if I would like to go to the beach. He put a chair in his car and drove me down to the deserted beach. He got the chair out of the car, put it in the middle of the beach, and drove off. He left me there for a couple of hours before returning to pick me up. This was the only time I went out on the whole retreat and it was really nice to sit by the sea.

Some of the meditations involved looking closely at all the different parts of our bodies, studying the changing sensations we were experiencing. He taught us about the elements and how they appear in our bodies and how to look out for them. He taught us releasing meditations too and how to let go of tensions within the body. We did regular Chi Kung which also helped enormously in letting go of tensions and stresses in the body and mind. We did a lot of marching and chanting too.

During this time I also learnt that with regular meditation our brain waves actually change and with it our thought patterns. This allows us to stop re-enacting the same old things over and over again. Knowing this I truly believe that it should be taught in prisons. It should also be included in schools with maybe some massage techniques too.

By the end of each day I was more than ready for my bed at 9pm. I slept very well all through the retreat.

Whatever time of day I went to my room, Kate was in the kitchen and I think she must have spent at least 12 hours a day chopping! The food she produced was absolutely amazing and she did all of that for no pay and this, I believe, is how all Buddhist retreats work. By serving it is said to improve one's Karma. I, for one, truly appreciated the hard work, love and kindness that emanated from all the volunteers. During my crying phase Kate even brought my meals to the room, knocking and leaving them at the door.

It was amazing how quickly I fitted into the routine having no real thoughts of my life away from the retreat. I did not miss Andrew or any other person or thing. It was so simple to just throw myself straight into the routine of meditating, exercising, eating, sleeping and learning.

As the last day approached Burgs said he would like, instead of a discourse, for us all to have some input. He said that it was not compulsory but he would like everyone to stand up at the front and say what the retreat had meant to them, making whatever comments they felt suitable at the time. He was going to invite the owners and the gardener in for this and then finish with a Metta Meditation. After that, he said, we could stay in the meditation hall in silence for as long as we wanted. After that we should go outside where we would be free to talk again if we chose to. He urged us to be mindful of others that may not want to talk for a while. One by one people got up and spoke (not everyone did this). People talked of different experiences but the common thread was that everyone had benefited greatly.

The owners said it had been a pleasure to have us there and went on to talk about their vision and dreams having come to fruition. They were quite clearly impressed with everything they had seen.

The gardener got up and said it had been a pleasure to provide our daily bread and see his produce, which he had tended with love and pride, made into such delicious meals. I understand that they had all been fed the same food as us.

It was very touching to me that quite a few people, including Burgs himself, commented on my bravery and determination throughout the week.

Despite me being obviously very shy at this point, Burgs egged me on to say something. He said I did not need to walk to the front but could just stand up where I was. He sensed that that was what I had been worried about but I did actually want to say something. It was a good, and possibly the only opportunity, I would have to thank people.

I told everyone how hard Kate had worked behind the scenes to provide us with 3 amazing meals every day. I also thanked everyone for their kindness and compassion towards me, which I assured them I had felt with gratitude. I also told the owners that I could feel the love and good intentions that had gone into the creation of the retreat. I talked briefly about my crying and thanked Burgs from the bottom of my heart for carrying me through it. I talked of the insights that time had taught me and of the feeling that a burden had been lifted from me.

Russell and Kate said how hard it had been when they heard me sobbing. They had desperately wanted to come and comfort me but Burgs had told them under no circumstances could they. He said it would have undone all the hard work that I had put in. Russell told me he just desperately wanted to come in and give me a hug. It was wonderful listening to the complete honesty everyone was sharing about the ups and downs they had gone through.

We then did a guided Metta Meditation and were told after that that we were free to go at any time. Finding myself not wanting to leave I just stayed within the silence I had grown used to. To my great surprise everyone stayed exactly where they were in the silence that the hall required of us all.

Gradually people started to get up and leave and after a while I followed. On leaving the hall I was expecting everyone to be outside talking but there was no-one there. Everyone was walking silently away in different directions. I had no intention of talking to anybody and headed straight for my room and lay down.

Slowly I could hear people going into the dining/communal area next door and I could hear a few voices. Within an hour or two it seemed like everyone was talking and to me it felt very intrusive and very loud. At this point I felt no inclination to talk or join anybody. I was staying another night and day and some of the people were returning home straight away. The noise of all the people next door was becoming deafening and making me feel very uncomfortable. Outside my room was the hallway which had a chair in it so I decided to go and sit on that as it was further away from the wall where the voices were coming from.

As I sat on the chair the bean bag lady appeared and launched straight into conversation, telling me she was a journalist and had come on the retreat to write about it. She started telling me about the state her house was in and how there wasn't an inch of space amongst all her stuff. She told me that to add to this there was an awful smell coming from the floor and she feared it was a dead rat and she would have to pull all the floorboards up. She then started telling me about a failed relationship at which point I asked her if she could please stop talking as I still needed to be in silence. I don't think she appreciated me saying this but I simply was not ready for any conversation, let alone an onslaught of her problems. I went back to my bedroom and lay down. Slowly the noise softened and I was able to go to sleep.

The next morning, when I awoke, there was only a handful of people left, Burgs, the volunteers, my friend Yvonne and the bean bag lady! Our flight was later that afternoon so Burgs suggested that we all get some kind of takeaway in the local town. The lovely Irish lady that had helped organise the retreat said she would pick us all up a Chinese meal.

When I offered to keep her company in the car the bean bag lady said she would like to come too. We got in the car with me in the front and the bean bag lady in the back and we went into town. Together they went in and got what everyone had asked for and the bean bag lady was given the bag to hold in the back of the car. Somehow she managed to spill a whole dish over the back seat by the time we got back to the retreat. Everyone rallied round, trying to mop it up but there remained a nasty stain and no doubt a smell. We brought the food to the table and everyone eagerly tucked in.

The bean bag lady announced to Burgs that during the week she had written him a poem and would like to take the opportunity to read it out loud to him and of course the audience she had in us. The poem was long and rambling but surprisingly quite good. She had written it as Burgs being Jesus' second coming. In her poem he was our teacher and saviour although many did not recognise him as this. She proudly came to the end of it and beamed at Burgs as if expecting praise. Burgs looked a bit awkward but graciously said he was flattered and thanked her. He then went on to say he was intrigued as to where and when she had written it. Yvonne joked she had written it on the cushion while meditating.

She left shortly afterwards and Burgs said she had completely missed the point by writing all through the retreat. She was the only person who admitted to have not gained anything from the retreat. She had seemed very surprised at all the experiences that everyone was talking about and how appreciative everyone was at what they had learned.

Whatever paper or magazine she wrote in I would imagine got another story completely to that of what we had all jointly experienced. It would have been good to have read it anyway. I sincerely hope that she has found something to calm her mind and her shambolic life. She missed a true gift there.

After lunch I asked the lady who owned the retreat if she could call a taxi for us. She said it would be her absolute pleasure to take us to the airport. We bundled our bags into her car and said our goodbyes. Burgs came out and wished us safe travels and said he hoped to see us again.

We arrived at the airport and the noise was so loud it made me glad we had planned to stay on another day as I would never have coped with it the day before. We boarded the plane and when we landed at Gatwick the noise was even louder.

Andrew was waiting for us and we went home, dropping Yvonne off on the way. It took me a while to get back to normal as general chit-chat all seemed very pointless. Andrew could not really understand what had happened and as it was all very personal it was very hard to explain. I am not sure I even wanted to explain at that point in time.

Burgs gave me many tools and life skills which I took away from his retreats. I still practice his meditations and Chi Kung to this day although nowhere near as often as I should. I am eternally grateful for his teachings and believe my life is greatly improved by them. These days I find myself much more accepting of my limitations and I enjoy the slower pace of life. A few of my friends who have frenetic, busy lives often comment that they like being with me as they are forced to slow down.

Often we see more by doing less.

In my old life, when I was fit, I am very well aware that I took my health for granted, always concentrating on the next new thing, place or adventure. Now I find myself much more in the present moment, appreciating every single thing that I do. I do believe that meditation has helped me reach this point.

I still refresh myself every now and again with one of Burgs' weekend retreats and I hope to do more full-on ones in the future.

Chapter 14 - Conventional Medicine and Surgery

The hospital appointments were still ongoing, even though I probably cancelled as many as I went to. The forms were very hard to fill in, asking what my pain was and ticking the face that I thought applied to me. These ranged from a full-on smiley face to a very pissed-off, screaming face. Being a glass-half-full sort of person, who had actually lost sight of what normality was, I would end up being told off by the grumpy, pessimistic rheumatologist who told me my answers were not realistic.

One day, while struggling with one of these forms one of the lovely nurses, Amanda, came over to chat to me. I told her I was struggling with these forms and how hospitals totally depressed me. It was obvious to her that the consultant and I did not get on and our personalities clashed. She said there was someone else she would like to introduce me to and rushed off. A few minutes later she came back with another consultant, Doctor Karen Walker-Bone, who I instantly liked. Karen told me not to worry about the forms and that she would love to take me on and she was happy if we could work together.

This was a new refreshing idea of working together with a consultant. This makes much more sense to me as, although the doctor has the theory and has studied for many years, it is the patient that fully understands the illness; he or she is living and experiencing it every single minute of every single day. There is room for both the patient and doctor to learn from each other and build up a mutually respectful relationship.

On telling her I was not happy to take the drug Methotrexate that had been prescribed to me she assured me that was fine. She saw me in her clinic right there and then. I told her my herbalist had said I had Polymyalgia Rheumatica and it would burn itself out. She gently examined me and said in her opinion she thought that unfortunately, I had Rheumatoid Arthritis. I had suspected this myself as the disease was getting worse, showing no signs of burning itself out.

She told me she was happy to take me on and have regular appointments with her, even if I still chose the alternative way above the conventional way. She was softly spoken, very warm and loving, unlike any conventional doctor I had come across.

She was the total opposite to the consultant I had been seeing. She assured me she was not going anywhere as she had signed a 25-year contract and I was welcome to contact her or Amanda at any time. She hugged me and told me she genuinely wanted to help me and get me better.

On talking to her staff and patients I learned that Karen Walker-Bone was a highly trained doctor who was loved and respected greatly. Another special relationship ensued. She told me she would book a proper consultation very soon.

At this consultation she told me about all the drugs available and how they worked. This list of drugs included anti-TNF drugs which were quite a new thing then. She went on to tell me that some of her patients had had amazing results taking them. TNF stands for Tumour Necrosis Factor and this, with RA, is over-produced in the body, causing inflammation and damage. Anti-TNF treatment blocks this thus reducing the inflammation. She said if a member of her family had this disease this is what she would be recommending.

This drug appealed to me more as it was addressing the disease from the root rather than just masking the symptoms. I trusted Karen and as nothing else seemed to be working I agreed that I would try this. I was given the option of weekly injections or to visit the hospital every 8 weeks where I would be given an infusion. The thought of injecting myself horrified me so I agreed to go to the hospital for an infusion and a date was set.

This infusion ended up taking all day as the staff were overworked and I also had to stay on for a few hours afterwards to make sure there were no nasty side-effects. After leaving the hospital I got home and went straight to bed. Over the next few days I felt absolutely dreadful with flu-like symptoms. I had a really bad constant headache and was completely lifeless. These symptoms wore off but there was no improvement in any of my joints.

I decided I would persevere as I know some drugs take a while to work. The next infusion was 2 weeks later with a third being 2 weeks after that. After that I was to have an infusion every 8 weeks. After about 4 infusions I came home as usual and went to bed feeling just as dreadful as I had the first time.

Pat, my carer arrived and she saw me lying in bed as white as my sheets and completely lifeless. I was awoken by her shaking me violently and shouting my name. She had literally thought I was dead! She had apparently been trying to wake me for quite a long time. When I next saw Karen Walker-Bone she said this was definitely NOT what was supposed to happen. It was meant to make me feel better not worse!

She recommended Humira which came in an injection and said I could have this done by a nurse at my local GP surgery. Andrew said he was quite happy to inject me and so it was agreed I go on Humira and this would be delivered to my home.

This was to be a subcutaneous injection and was to be put into the fatty tissue just beneath the skin. It must be given in an area where there is enough fatty tissue. The best places for this are the abdomen (this was my choice as I have more fat there!) top of the thighs or buttocks.

The injections arrived and Andrew injected one into my tummy while I closed my eyes and cringed! This became habit and slowly but surely I began to feel better. My energy levels were up and I became much more interested in life. Unfortunately I was still struggling to walk and I could still only go out in a wheelchair.

One morning, after a few months of Andrew injecting me, he was outside in his workshop when the time came for the injection. I had the sudden thought that I could do it myself and went and got the syringe.

Sure enough I pinched some skin put it slowly in and slowly withdrew it. YES I had done it! This was a great feeling of achievement and I felt very proud of myself. It was something else on my list of things I did not have to ask Andrew to do for me. It was another step towards being independent. After a while I realised that it was actually easier to do it myself, as I was in control and was aware of how it needed to go in to keep it as pain free as possible. The syringes got better with time too with springs in them so you no longer had to withdraw the needle. Andrew came in later to remind me that he needed to give me my injection. When I told him I had done it myself he laughed and did not believe me. It took a while to convince him I really had but he was pleased although he said it had never bothered him doing it.

At my next appointment with Karen, I proudly told her that I was now doing my own injections. She had known my aversion to needles so was very surprised and impressed. She said she was very proud of me.

Karen said she was becoming very concerned at how much weight I had lost and said I looked tiny in my wheelchair. The chair was a big one and to be honest I knew absolutely nothing about wheelchairs and just assumed they were all the same. I certainly didn't know they came in different sizes! It was something I had never had to spend much thought on, like everything else that comes with disability.

She asked if I would go and get an x-ray of my hips as she felt that with the time I had been on the drugs she would have expected me to be a bit more mobile by now. She gave me an x-ray form and said I could come straight back to her clinic where she could get it up on her screen and we could look at it together.

When my x-ray came up she gasped and said "Oh Poppet, they are completely gone. No wonder you are in so much pain. It is just bone on bone." She told me that no drugs or herbs under the sun could sort this out and that I needed to have both my hips replaced. She had such a loving way about her and she had tears in her eyes as she told me. She really did feel like a friend to me and the fact that she did genuinely care meant so much to me the whole time I was under her care. She cared for me holistically which is rare in my experience for a doctor. She told me once that she wanted to be a doctor from the age of two. She was born to be a doctor and I am honoured to have met her and built such a beautiful doctor-patient relationship with her. I am glad too that it was her that told me this devastating news.

I burst into tears and she gave me a hug saying that she would see me through this and slowly I calmed down.

Literally, the week before (synchronicity at it's best) I had seen an amazing surgeon on a TV program, Hugh Apthorp, who was replacing hips differently to the conventional way. He was leaving smaller scars and the recovery time was greatly reduced. It was, incredibly, minimal invasive surgery for a whole hip replacement. I started actually watching the operation but I have never been good at blood and gore and it was looking very brutal with hammers and saws so I turned the TV off and picked up a book to read instead. The memory of this truly amazing man luckily stayed with me.

This man was a hero and his patients were literally leaving the same day as their operation. It was truly remarkable and people were coming from as far away as Scotland (to Sussex) to have him operate on them. Karen had not heard of this surgeon and told me he was by no means the nearest. She said she knew of good surgeons and would normally have written to them but she told me she would be happy to write to him. She said she obviously could not guarantee the outcome or whether he would agree to operate on me but she would try her best to convince him.

Before long I had a letter with an appointment to see him. He was a lovely man and said he would be happy to operate on me but it was on the condition that my bone density was good enough. To test this I needed an x-ray which he arranged and said he would write to me with the results.

As I was in such a bad way I was convinced that he would not be able to do the operation and that my bone density would not be good enough. Very soon after the x-ray a letter arrived saying that all was well and an appointment had been made for 6 months time at the hospital of my choice. He worked at 2 hospitals, one was the general and the other was the arthritic hospital where I went for hydrotherapy. This was obviously my choice as it was nearest to me, in a beautiful setting and I had made friends with the physiotherapists including my dear friend Chris. This hospital had a lovely policy where all the patients got up for meals and the patients and staff ate together in a wonderful canteen where they actually served decent food. It would mean that I would be looked after by people I already knew and who liked me and I would be eating with them too. I was also familiar with the surroundings so it felt a lot less daunting than the big hospital I had seen the surgeon at, which was a long way from home. As I don't like hospitals (who does?) this was a much nicer option.

This was exciting but also very scary and daunting as I had only ever had a few very minor operations in the whole of my life. My family and friends, I think , were more excited about the prospect than me. I was petrified!

In the meantime my pain was getting worse and worse to the point that painkillers were not even touching it. Karen prescribed some morphine patches for me which did help the pain but did strange things to my mind. It made me paranoid and anxious thinking that I should be tidying up and doing housework when in fact I was totally incapable of doing anything. When Andrew came up to see me I thought he was going to hit me for not having done anything. This was totally ludicrous as he would never have done anything to hurt me in any way.

As the time got nearer I just could not cope with the pain so phoned the general hospital where Hugh Apthorp worked. I told them I didn't care any more where the operation took place, I just needed it as soon as possible as the pain had become completely unbearable. My hips were completely locked, my legs permanently apart and when I did manage to move my hips they made the most dreadful crunching noise and the pain was the worst I have ever experienced. They assured me that if a cancellation came up I would be the first person they rang.

A few weeks after that conversation the hospital rang me and said there had been a cancellation on the 21st December at the general hospital and would I like to have the operation on that day? Although this was only a month before my original appointment at the arthritic hospital, I jumped at it and said YES I would take it! By this time he could have performed it in the car park for all I cared!

Looking back I am glad in a way that my hospital care was with strangers rather than people I knew as it was not the most dignified time of my life!

As the date loomed nearer I became more and more scared (I think the morphine had a part to play in this). By this time I weighed 7 stone which was very underweight for me. My muscles had wasted and I was very weak, making me feel that it would be impossible to come through this operation. Lots of people were ringing me and wishing me well and telling great tales of how they knew people who had had their hips replaced and were now leading normal lives – walking, hiking, swimming etc.

One of Andrew's customers enquired after me as he had not seen me for ages. He was very shocked to hear that I was now bed-ridden awaiting hip replacements. He asked Andrew if he thought I would mind if he and some of his congregation prayed for me.

Andrew said he knew I wouldn't mind and in fact would be very grateful. About a week later I got a parcel in the post with a card and some anointed cloth. This man had prayed with others for my recovery and anointed this cloth for me to have. It smelled absolutely divine and was such an appreciated gesture of love. I received a further 65 cards and presents wishing me good luck.

My friend, Jessie, rang me to tell me that someone she knew, who had not been able to walk when she had last seen him, had recently had his hips replaced and was now doing really well and going on long hikes. She said she was really excited for me and couldn't wait to see me after my operation as she knew I was going to be completely different.

She had been a real rock all through my illness often phoning me with funny stories and sending me lovely cards when she knew I was faltering. One day she had sent me a big yellow smiley card with a newspaper cutting inside a letter. The newspaper cutting was of the front page of her local newspaper with a photo of a man that had been a mutual friend of ours in our teens. He was now a campaigner and activist for the legalisation of cannabis for medical use. The photo was of him with a banner looking totally wrecked. She joked that it really wasn't a good advert for promoting cannabis and if she was going to campaign for that she would have taken a photo before she got stoned! She always made me laugh and this was no exception. I still have this letter and newspaper clipping and it still makes me laugh. We had a similar sense of humour and I always appreciated her funny stories and her friendship.

The sea of love that surrounded me made me feel warm, loved and protected despite the pain I was in. The anointed cloth I had received stayed in bed with me, and I smelt it all the time sensing the compassion, love and time spent by these beautiful people praying for someone (me) that they did not even know. I sniffed that cloth until the smell had completely gone!

Russell had told Burgs that I was due to have my hips replaced and he asked to know the exact day. He told me he would be sending out healing to me throughout the day. He had a photo of me which he said he would place on his shrine. This was a great comfort to me and also, knowing that other friends would be thinking and praying for me too.

This sounds silly now, I know, but I made sure everyone I loved knew how much I loved them before I went into hospital as I was sure I was going to die!

Finally the time came and it was requested that I go into the hospital the evening before my operation. Andrew drove me there and wheeled me to my ward in my wheelchair. He made sure I was comfortable and stayed with me for a little while. When he left I felt very alone and very scared. The ward I was in was a geriatric ward mainly filled with old senile women so I knew I was going to get no comfort from them. The night brought loud snoring, screams and nurses regularly coming in with commodes and to change beds. The smells were horrendous and were actually making me feel quite sick.

All in all it was a very bad night's sleep for me. One lesson I learned from this is to ALWAYS take earplugs into hospital and it is always at the top of my list if I need to go into hospital to stay overnight.

When I finally did get off to sleep properly it was early morning and the lights came on and the noisy hospital day had begun. Observations were being carried out and breakfasts were being served.

There was no breakfast for me as I was Nil By Mouth. The nurse came round and informed me that I was first on the surgeon's list and my operation would begin at 8.30 am. She needed to shower me and cover my body with Betadine in preparation for my operation. This is a browny yellow liquid scrub to kill bacteria and prevent contamination and infection of the surgical site. Her doing this made me feel useless and very undignified and I felt quite upset.

After the shower, she put a gown on me and I went back to my bed and pulled the curtains around me. Sitting on the bed I just quietly sobbed, convinced that I was going to die that day and really did not want to. I had never been so scared.

A nurse peeped around the curtain and saw me crying and asked in a very no-nonsense way why I was crying. On telling her I thought I was going to die she told me not to be so silly and left leaving me feeling like a silly little girl. Laying down I tried really hard to pull myself together and stop crying. After doing some breathing exercises I tried to tell myself that all was going to be well and managed to calm myself down a bit.

Soon after that the porters came to take me down to the theatre. I remember looking at the corridors I was being wheeled through thinking they would be the last things I saw.

The anaesthetists tried to reassure me that everything was going to be OK and they would be there looking after me and that the surgeon's work was amazing. The surgeon came in and told me he would try his best to replace both of my hips but that it was possible he would run out of time and would only be able to do one on that day. The anaesthetist gave me an epidural, and then nothing....

When I woke up in the recovery room the first question I asked was whether the surgeon had managed to replace both of my hips. The man looking after me told me he had and that the whole operation had gone very well. That was a relief.

Not only had I had both my hips replaced, I was also alive!

After a short time I was wheeled back to the ward and was told the physiotherapists would come and see me soon and get me up walking! There were still a lot of tubes attached to me, a catheter and drains coming from my hips with bags to collect blood. There was a button I could press if I was in pain. This was a way for me to self-administer morphine and the nurse assured me that due to the set-up it was impossible for me to overdose.

Incredibly I did not need much morphine as I don't think anything could have been worse than the continuous excruciating pain I had been in before the operation. That pain had gone and been replaced with another, post-operation type pain. The nurse said that she had noticed that her patients who suffered from Rheumatoid Arthritis always had less pain relief post-operation and she believed it was because we'd had to endure more pain and we had built up a higher pain threshold.

Another nurse came to see me to do my observations and asked me if I had taken arnica beforehand and I said yes I had been taking the tablets for quite a few weeks beforehand. She said she could tell because I only had a little bruising and she was used to seeing people's bodies black and blue. Later on she came back with a tube of arnica cream which everyone is given post-operation. I was amazed that this was recognised within the NHS. Yes, I do know it is homeopathy and am happy to take the standard things which are well used and recognised and I have no horrible side effects from them.

The physiotherapists came round in the afternoon and had me up walking around the ward on a Zimmer frame once they had mastered where all my tubes and bags were going to go. It was the best walking I had achieved in 4 years and I felt elated and hopeful once more. They sat me up in a chair and left.

Soon after this my godmother, Sylvia, arrived, expecting to see me in bed very poorly. Because of this she did not recognise me sitting in my chair and walked straight past me! I was on a high from the drugs and the fact that I had walked so well earlier and I called out to her. She could not believe the difference in me and did not believe that I had been up walking. To prove it to her to I got up on my Zimmer frame and walked around the ward. She looked on amazed and delighted.

Before the operation the surgeon had warned me that due to my posture and my back being so bent not to expect to be straight afterwards. He also said that with bilateral replacements it was not always possible to get the legs both the same length again. He said if this happened I would have to wear adapted shoes with one of them raised.

Luckily he had done the best job possible on me. I was upright and my legs perfectly balanced. My scars are tiny, to the point where I even forget they are there, and my hips work perfectly.

That man is a star and will be my hero for the rest of my life. I send out a thank you to him every single day. He gave me my life back. One day a few months later when I went to the arthritic hospital I overheard a few of the staff talking about my surgeon saying how flash he was and he must be earning a fortune as he drove such a flash car, it was either a

Porsche or a Ferrari, I can't remember. I couldn't help myself and interrupted them even though I had been eavesdropping. I said he deserved it more than anyone and the huge salary too, he was highly trained, worked long hours and was giving the best thing to people that anyone could give … their lives. Not only did he deserve a huge salary but recognition and respect for his amazing work. They looked a bit embarrassed and changed the subject.

My prayers are that he lives a long, happy and healthy life and carries on doing the amazing and life-changing work he does right up to his retirement and beyond.

From all of this, and no doubt the drugs, and of course the relief, I was buzzing and on a high. I rang all my friends saying I felt wonderful. My poor friends were all bombarded with my enthusiasm that day but I am sure it was better than the pained, frail and scared friend they had heard a few days prior to that. I am always blown away at how one day to the next can sometimes be so contrasting. The day before I had been sobbing my heart out thinking I was going to die!

Andrew came to visit and brought me some gingerbread men he had made and he had put silver balls in their hips. That cheered me up, he was so good at making things and adding silly quirky little touches and this was a typical example of that. He always made cards and makes his own Christmas cards which many people say they look forward to with eager anticipation each year. He was obviously happy that my operation had been successful and I was already walking about.

After they had left a nurse suggested I got back into bed as she would like to give me a blood transfusion. The blood that had drained from my hips was simply going to be transfused back into me by a drip as I was slightly anaemic. She set this up and left it to slowly drip back into me. Shortly after she left the bag, which was over my head, burst, literally covering my head, face and body in blood. Someone pressed their bell and the nurse came in and freaked out, seeing me covered in blood. She was very relieved when she learnt where the blood had come from. She cleaned me up and I was laughing, thinking the whole thing was really funny. This probably was to do with all the drugs I had had. The blood transfusion never did take place after that.

The physiotherapists came back the next day and said they would get me on crutches and as soon as I could get up and down 5 steps I would be able to go home.

Several visitors came to see me with flowers and gifts. Lorraine came to see me bringing beautiful smellies. She massaged some cream into my arms and I told her my arm pits were really smelly. Bless her she got a flannel out of my bag and some shower gel and washed them for me and put my deodorant on. She laughs at me when I bring that up as an example of our good friendship and feels it really was nothing. She is so good at doing the practical things that need doing and I love her for that. I still claim that the act of washing my armpits was beyond the call of friendship! Leaving me clean and fresh-smelling was a very special gift. After an operation there are so many weird smells going on so that really was so appreciated.

Although most people went home the following day, I was not allowed to because of the severe muscle wastage that had happened over the last few years and they wanted me to be to be able to haul myself up the bed before they let me go.

Christmas was approaching and it became quite apparent that they were trying to empty the wards and were saying that I could go home. My confidence was not good enough as we had a lot of outside steps and a very steep staircase inside the house and I was really not sure, at this stage, whether I was capable of doing all this. A compromise was reached and they agreed to arrange for an ambulance to take me home on Christmas Eve and the paramedics agreed that they would carry me up the stairs on a stretcher.

Andrew had assumed that I would not be home for Christmas so our friend, Jane, had kindly invited him to join her family for Christmas dinner. Because of this we had very little festive food in the house but Jane, bless her, ended up making 2 extra dinners for Andrew to bring home so that we could enjoy a Christmas dinner together. The dinner was perfectly home-cooked and very gratefully received by both of us.

My dear friend Jessie had been ill for a few months now and had recently been diagnosed with cancer of the lung and liver and was seriously ill in hospital. My friend Annie had told me that she had been told that it didn't look like she was going to live much longer.

On Boxing Day I told Andrew that I needed to go and see her. He said I was not ready and I needed to wait until I was stronger and more confident and he would maybe take me the following week. He said I needed to think of myself. I had just had major surgery and needed to take things easy and take care. I replied that if he didn't take me I would have to call a taxi as I absolutely had to see her as it could possibly be the last opportunity I had. He thought I was being over-dramatic but I had a really strong feeling that I had to see her that day so he backed down and agreed to take me and although it completely wore me out I am so glad I insisted as she died a few days later.

When we arrived at the hospital, she was in a side ward and I went in there on my crutches. She could not get up and I could not bend down so she came up with a special Angie/Jessie kiss where she kissed her hand and touched me and I kissed my hand and touched her. It was a very special exchange between us.

She was still trying to smile and joke as she always had, although it was obvious that the drugs were making her paranoid and confused and she was in pain. I don't think she believed herself that she was going to die but looking at her, I think I knew.

We had always joked that we were invincible; I so wish she had been right and that she was still here today with her bright sunny beautiful spirit. Dean was there and had been with her all the time she was there, sleeping on a mattress next to her bed. He was talking about her going to a hospice to get better. I felt so sorry for him as the devotion and love he had for her was so clear.

She was delighted to see me up on my crutches and I am glad that she at least saw me on the mend before she died. I will never forget her optimism and huge life-force and will always miss that. She was a ray of sunshine in mine and many other people's lives and the full church at her funeral was testament to that.

We were not there very long as Jessie was getting anxious and confused. I tried to assure her that it was the effects of the morphine as I had had the same thing before I was in hospital. I think, and hope, that it did register and make her feel calmer.

When we left and were walking up the outer hallway I heard Dean calling me. I turned round and he was running after us. He asked me what I thought about Jessie's predicament and I honestly replied that I didn't think it was looking good. He looked shocked at my reply so obviously thought she was going to recover. Jessie was a fighter but it was going to take too big a fight for her now to come back I thought. I didn't voice my thoughts but just gave him a big hug and told him to take care. On asking Andrew what he thought he agreed with me that it was not looking good. My heart was breaking for the loss that was going to follow.

I continued to do my exercises and went from 2 crutches down to one crutch and then down to sticks, to one stick, to no sticks! Alistair, my Bowen therapist, passed me onto one of his pupils so he could take on someone else in greater need as that is what he did best. She came regularly to do Bowen on me and having been taught by Alistair she was of course good and I believe that this helped accelerate my healing.

Chapter 15 - Wind In My Hair

In the whole 4 years of being more or less bed-ridden I had kept my car on the drive and kept up all the insurance payments and had it MOT'd each year. This to some people was totally crazy, but to me, my car had always symbolised my freedom and by keeping it legal and on the drive was keeping the hope alive that one day I would miraculously drive it again and have my freedom back.

Andrew borrowed my car one evening to go to a gig. The weather was not good and the gig was a long way to travel to and my car was the safer option for this journey so I was happy for him to take it.

When I awoke at midnight I was surprised that he was not home but was not unduly worried as he was a night-owl and was always the last to leave anywhere so I went back to sleep. A few of the pubs in Sussex were known to have lock-ins so I thought maybe this had happened. However on awaking again at 3am and finding he was still not home I laid awake worrying. Soon after that the phone rang and I got up and downstairs on my crutches, shaking and worried as I fully expected it to be the hospital or the police saying that Andrew was either seriously injured or had been killed in an accident.

When I answered the phone it was such a huge relief to hear Andrew's voice at the end of it. He had had an accident and slid on some ice and had ended up in a ditch in the middle of the Sussex countryside. He had walked some distance in the freezing cold to a house a few miles up the road. His biggest concern was that he had trashed my car but I was so relieved that he was OK that I really didn't care about the car. He had also called the RAC who were going to bring him home.

My car was written off by the insurance company and they paid me a very reasonable amount of money considering it was a very old car.

At this point in time I was starting to drive again. Having always wanted a soft-top cabriolet car I decided that after 4 years in bed I deserved some fun and some wind in my hair. My friend Chris had given me a taster of it and I wanted that for myself.

Andrew and I looked at various cabriolet cars. A few of these were brand new. Andrew said he felt that I should not waste my money on a new one as it was probable, as I had not driven for so long, that I would get a few dings and scrapes on it.

I finally chose one which was quite old but in really good condition with low mileage. I bought this at the end of March and the sun shone every day all through the summer that year. There were very few days that I did not have the roof down.

One of my first journeys in this car on my own was to Lorraine's house in Seaford. Arriving with my hair in a cap and the roof off, she looked out of the window and started crying. She told me that it felt like she had her old friend back at last!

My birthday is in April and Andrew and I booked a helicopter ride around Snowdonia. We drove from Sussex to Wales with the wind in our hair and then flew over Snowdonia and stayed in a wonderful guest house on Anglesey. The time was a joyous one for us both. We had suffered for so long and were now out doing adventurous things again. It felt good. Life was most definitely looking up.

The day was warm and sunny so we went on the beach and I walked across the beach to paddle in the sea. Overcome with emotion I started crying. The sea and the water mean so much to me and I had often been sad that I would never be able to go in the sea again. Laying in bed I had done so many meditative visualisations of being on the beach and walking along, paddling in the sea.

The reality, at one point, was definitely looking like I would never be able to physically do this ever again. So to be here, actually doing it in real life was completely overwhelming. The tears were of sheer joy and relief.

There were many more moments like this one in the coming weeks, months and years, and to this day I revel in simple acts that most people take for granted.

To be able to shower myself is one of these things, kicking leaves, having a hug and even eating a meal are some of the things that were once impossible for me to do. I never take any of these things for granted now, knowing that they could be taken away from me again at any time. The gratitude I feel for my life is in every moment of every day and it is huge.

Sometimes I think I am probably happier than most able-bodied fit people as I am appreciating every single moment. Occasionally I find myself observing other people and am aware that within their frenetic lives rushing around chasing their tails there is no real presence or joy. It makes me actually grateful to have been forced to slow down and be fully present in the here and now.

Buying this car was the best thing I ever did. My whole life had been opened up again and I had wind in my hair and the blissful freedom to go out on my own, visit friends, or just simply drive and enjoy. Life was actually becoming exciting again.

After having my hips replaced, the new drugs did not solve everything and I still had some fatigue and mobility issues but to me just having some of my previous life back was a huge blessing. It meant that I was now able to plan things and make arrangements and my life started to be my own again. This was very, very, exciting to me.

Chapter 16 - Putting Something Back

Slowly but surely some of my energy started to return and my walking became easier. A lot of my other joints still hurt and I was still in some pain but my life started to become much more enjoyable and I started going out independently. After a while I found myself thinking about work again and began to wonder what I could do. My mobility was still greatly restricted and my energy levels still quite low so whatever I chose would have to be part time.

One day I was wandering through Shrewsbury (a town we now lived near) and I walked into Oxfam where they had a notice asking for volunteers. On impulse I enquired and the lady got the manageress out from the back. She asked me to fill in a form there and then. She said she would chase up the references straight away and could I start the following week?! She asked if I could work 2 afternoons a week and said I would be working with the other manageress, Geri.

On returning home I told Andrew I had got myself a job as a volunteer in a charity shop. He initially thought I was messing around but when I insisted it was true he was happy that I was going to be doing something different and was very supportive.

The following week I got dressed up nicely and drove myself to the park-and-ride outside the town. When I got on the bus I rang my friend Lorraine and told her I was on a bus going to work. She said she felt tearful because she never thought it would be possible for me to be able to do this. It was quite an emotional phone call as I was recalling in my head the time when my whole body had been in excruciating pain and I could not dress or feed myself. It was at that point I had told her I was going to commit suicide. We both felt very happy and proud of how far I had come. It was so good to be sharing this moment with her.

On getting off the bus I walked, somewhat nervously, into Oxfam to meet Geri.

Geri was so warm and friendly and obviously very happy to have me on board. She said that it was important to her that all her volunteers were happy. She therefore liked them to be doing the jobs that suited them best. She went on to show me all the various jobs that needed to be done and I told her that being on the till appealed to me the most. I had often been told that I was good with people and I generally liked being sociable so I was really looking forward to being a front-of-house person. She said that that was really good as most of her volunteers did not actually like being on the till, preferring to be out the back of the shop, sorting and pricing the goods. A lot of the volunteers there, as with other charity shops, are volunteering because they have some kind of disability whether it be physical or mental. It is good work experience, often as a stepping stone to something else. Geri told me that quite a few of her volunteers were not capable of using the till and it scared them and so did interaction with the shoppers. This made me very happy as I had done a bit of shop work when I was younger and really enjoyed it.

Geri immediately started me on the till and before I knew it, the hours had flown by. Over the next few weeks and months I met and made friends with both staff and customers and found myself having a lot of fun. I started to really look forward to these afternoons.

Geri was an amazing boss, encouraging us all to change the shop around as we saw fit and making our own displays. This meant that everyone was happy and enthusiastic. Geri had loads of energy and a great sense of humour and we all buzzed around her and the shop always looked amazing. It looked more like an upmarket dress agency than a charity shop. It was really wonderful to be part of this team. I found my confidence growing and a new-found pride in what I was achieving.

Periodically a lady who worked on all the world emergency crises – floods, famines etc would come in and do a slide-show. She talked about the incredible work she and her colleagues did.

These slide-shows were so informative and she told us how humbled she was time and time again by the people affected. She worked with a team of people, including emergency specialists, who were all quite clearly totally awesome. She told us that she had a small bag always packed as she could literally be called out any time morning or night. Disasters are never conveniently timed! She said she found it humbling when people didn't have anything that they were happy to share whatever they had. She showed us a photo of a bowl of rice being shared between 10 people.

She educated me on the ethos of Oxfam and the great thing about this charity is they don't just give support and aid and then leave. Their work is not short-term but looks ahead long-term and gives people opportunities to help themselves. They can become self-sufficient, which gives them an income and pride. They are forward thinking. She talked about the importance of selling the gift cards to people and showed us real life stories of how these had helped people. The purchase of a card buys a goat, solar energy, safe water etc, and not only saves lives but gives people a helping hand to help themselves. These people would often risk their own lives to get to the victims of these disasters and I found myself totally in awe of their work. She took photos of some of these people and said they were on our price tags which I had never actually registered before.

When disasters happen Oxfam go straight into overdrive raising funds. We would have tins brought straight to our shop. All this money goes straight to that crisis. People would obviously hear pretty much straight away from the news and it was uplifting how many people came in to donate, sometimes very large amounts. The public response and generosity was good to see and even children would come in with their pocket money. It was impressive how many young people would come in and stuff notes into the tin. Times like this do bring out the best in people and it was heart-warming to see this first hand. There are a lot of truly compassionate people out there.

In my time working in the shop there were two major disasters.

There was the Haiti earthquake which killed over 220,000 people with over 300,000 people injured. The immediate response from Oxfam provided aid for 2.4 million people. They provided clean water, shelter and basic sanitation, and set up canteens to provide hot meals.

And then there were the Pakistan floods. This covered one fifth of Pakistan's land which is a huge area. It affected 20 million people and killed 2000. She showed us loads of pictures of this and told us that one of the workers had been killed trying to reach the victims. Some of the photos were of people that had lost everything but incredibly they still had amazing beautiful smiles. Some of those faces are still etched in my mind.

She went on to tell us she was in awe of us volunteers, saying that without our work in the shops, raising valuable money, none of this humanitarian work would happen. This, for me, was a real light-bulb moment. She broke down costs of medical supplies, food, sanitation etc. It made me realise that by volunteering in Oxfam I was literally saving lives and this was a great feeling.

I had initially volunteered for my own reasons — as a kind of rehabilitation back into society, to build my confidence and to make new friends in a new area I found myself in. The reality was so much more than that. I had achieved all the things I had set out to do but was also a small part of something very big and incredibly special.

Over the next few years I learned a lot more about Oxfam and what an absolutely amazing and organised charity they are and am very proud to have been part of it. Working there also made me feel better as I had taken a lot out in previous years especially from the NHS. It felt like it was a way of putting something back. For me that is how the Universe works, when someone does a kind act you may not be able to return it to them but you can repay it by passing on a good deed to someone else.

During my four years in bed there was not a lot of opportunity to give and many people had given me their time, love and expertise. By working in Oxfam I did give a lot back. I always tried to help the customers and be kind to them and the staff, and being a volunteer raised money to help save lives. Good deeds are never wasted. Give when you can and graciously receive when you need to. People do actually like to help and it is often a way to give them a purpose. Before I was ill I was fiercely independent and hated asking for help or accepting any offers of help. On finding myself unable to do most things I had no option but to ask for help. Without help I would have died. Pride can be so stupid, if I need help now I find it quite easy to ask and realise that people actually do want to help. Admitting to being vulnerable is a good thing and shows your humanness and is, I realise now, much more attractive. Being ill has made me surrender to help and made me much softer and also much more compassionate and understanding of other people's needs.

One day, just before Christmas, I took some of my home-made Christmas biscuits into the shop to share with the staff. There was a new lady in there called Amy Apple whom I had not met before. She admired the Ecuadorian cardigan I was wearing and told me she had once lived up the road from where they made these jumpers. She had a rucksack on and was just about to go to the train station to go to Wales to visit her family. She and I hit it off immediately and when I next went into work I was told she had asked to work alongside me. A great friendship was born.

After a while Amy Apple said she was leaving as a place had come up in the market. She made wire-work jewellery and was going to sell it on the stall. She said I was welcome to join her and share the costs if I wanted to sell something alongside her.

After thinking on this for a while and as I have always loved crystals I asked her how she felt about me selling them alongside her jewellery. She was really happy with this idea and said that my crystals would definitely complement her jewellery.

Together we went to an amazing crystal ware-house and I purchased £1000 worth of goods, varying from small tumblestones and items of jewellery to massive amethyst church crystals.

A friend of Amy Apple's lent us a Wurlitzer jukebox and before long we had a beautiful, vibrant stall. It was a permanent stall with shutters that we could draw down and lock at the end of each day. We called our little shop Silver Lining and when I think of those times it brings back happy memories of a lovely friendship.

Chapter 17 - Conclusion

The journey I have been on so far, since becoming ill, has been incredibly hard and totally unbearable at times. Despite this, I believe I have been truly blessed. Suffering, I have learned, is our biggest teacher and I think I have gained wisdom way beyond my years.

I have learned that to survive I had to turn inwards, which is where the true healing happens. I have been blessed to meet the most beautiful people I would never have met had I not been ill. These people have both taught and humbled me beyond anything I could ever have imagined.

The Angelic Experience I had one night (some may say I was dreaming or hallucinating but I can only relay it as I witnessed it) changed my life forever, bringing forth from that day what I call Earth Angels to heal and teach me. I have learned to totally trust that the right people come into our lives at exactly the right time and we really are only given what we can cope with.

I feel a great sense of pride at how far I have come through so many difficulties. I think I am a much nicer, calmer, more compassionate human being now than I was at the beginning of this journey. The awareness of my angels being around has stayed with me and I often ask them for help and I always remember to thank them too. Knowing they are there beside me brings me peace and I always feel looked after.

My Buddhist teacher, Burgs, as well as teaching me meditation and Chi Kung, also taught me the most important lesson of forgiveness. It took a long time, but with a lot of hard work, I have managed to forgive my mother and my sister.

My sister and I made up and I realised, after talking to her, that we both see things very differently. She convinced me that she truly believed that she thought everything she did was right at the time. On discussing our childhoods we even have different memories, views and opinions on most events. The time I spent with her was very enlightening to me and helped me understand her a bit better. By then we had both learnt a lot about the effects of adoption and the primal wound and I felt a lot of compassion towards her. She moved away, surprisingly to Somerset, and we are no longer in contact with each other. I think we both realised that we see life so differently. She remains in my daily Metta Meditations and I sincerely wish her well and happy.

Andrew and I split up after a 12-year relationship. I am forever grateful to him for sharing this part of my life with me and taking on the hard journey of looking after me. He literally did everything for me for a long time and I don't know how, or if, I would have survived without him.

When I told my consultant Karen that we had split up she told me that sadly she sees this happen to many of her patients. She said that when a relationship becomes a patient/carer relationship and the patient starts to recover, often the changes and dynamics within the relationship shift to make it impossible to continue as it was before. I found myself desperately needing to spread my wings and fly, by which time Andrew had a large restoration project that was taking up most of his time.

We remain good friends and have both since met new partners.

I am now happily married to Max and have two wonderful stepsons. Although I still have some mobility issues I am happier than I have ever been and am having lots of fun.

My life is mainly full of love and laughter and I still revel in all the simple things that life offers. Max and I love travelling and we have been for many long holidays. The last one being to Spain for 5 weeks in our motorhome.

We go to Spain now every winter as the warmth helps with RA and we have also discovered the natural hot springs dotted around Spain. To me these hot springs are heavenly and help my mobility enormously. Max and I spend many an hour wallowing in them. The natural minerals within these springs are renowned for their healing properties and people flock from around the world to benefit from them.

I am now a qualified Reiki practitioner and Max and I are in the process of setting up positivity life-coaching retreats. We practice gratitude on a daily basis, telling each other what we are grateful for every morning. We find this is the best way to go on to have a happy and fulfilled day. I have also kept up the practice of affirmations which are forever changing.

We also have a file we call our laughter file, into which we put funny cards, photos, memories, anything that has made us laugh. When one or both of us are down we get that out and it never fails to make us laugh.

My healthy diet continues and I still juice.

I can now swim many lengths.

With hindsight (oh, what a marvellous thing that is!) I would no longer trust anyone who claims they could cure me. Instead of giving them huge amounts of money I would suggest that, upon the cure, I give them 10 times the amount they were asking. No cure, no money! The people that said they could help me rather than cure me were the ones I found to be kinder and more genuine, and they are the ones that I respect to this day and have remained in contact with.

I still believe in miracles and remain positive but am a bit less ready to pay for them!

Luckily I retain a good sense of humour and can laugh about all these things now. I have always seen life as a series of stories which all have humour in them. Admittedly it is not always easy to see the humour. However, as I get older, I think I am getting better at seeing it in everything at the time. My sense of humour (some would say warped) has definitely helped carry me through the difficult times and continues to do so.

My whole intention of writing this book is that anyone reading it (especially if sick) is inspired to carry on whatever their journey is, recognise it as a challenge, grow through the pain and remember Light ALWAYS Follows Darkness. Always keep hope alive. Although a lot of things I tried did not work I am still grateful for them as they gave me hope and taught me lots of things, even if they were lessons I didn't want at the time. They were all valuable. Life is not always easy.

I literally have gone from a dark place of not being able to do anything for myself, being house-bound, and not wanting to live, to a life full of love, joy and travel. In fact my life is better and happier than it has ever been with an inner contentment to boot!

In the last few years I have found out about my birth family. My mum had Rheumatoid Arthritis, which is a better theory of why I now have it than some of the other many theories I was given. That has been interesting for me too as I often thought that illnesses through the generations were more about habits copied than genes. To simplify this I give the example of blaming being fat on the fact that your mum is fat when it is in fact because you all eat a lot, but as I now know even that is complex.

I still believe that it was the stress that brought my illness on but now also believe that I was always going to be prone to getting it as it runs through the family. My birth sister also has it but in a much milder form.

Sadly my birth mum died at the age of 48 so I never had the chance to meet her, although I do have a photo. We are so alike in looks and it is good to have a photo of someone that looks like me (something only an adoptee understands). I have also met my brother and his family and they are all lovely ... good stuff!

My journey continues, as everyone's does, and all I can do is go forward optimistically believing in myself and other people and try and be the best person I can be.

There are always challenges and good and bad times as we go through the seasons of life and I hope that I embrace them all and come through happier and stronger. Hope is the key word, keep it always in your heart. Life does get better.

As I was coming to the end of this book my dear friend Lin shared a lovely quote, as she does every morning, on Facebook and it spoke to me beautifully, summarising everything. It is from the the *Anam Cara* book by John O'Donohue, and as Max and I based our wedding vows around this book it felt very apt to be ending with it, so I am sharing it with you all here:-

> *When you cease to fear your solitude, a new creativity awakens within you. Your forgotten or neglected wealth begins to reveal itself.*

You come home to yourself and learn to rest within.
Thoughts are our inner senses.

Infused with silence and solitude, they bring out the
mystery of inner landscape

May you be blessed always.

With all my love, Angie xx

May all beings be happy.

Acknowledgements

I have tried not to name and shame anyone in this book, keeping the people that did not help me anonymous. The people that I have named have given me permission to do so.

I have so many people to thank and feel so blessed to have had them all in my life in the roles they played.

Firstly, I would like to thank Andrew Norman. Thank you Andrew for your care, love and patience you gave me over the years. Thank you for the yummy organic food and juices you served me every single day with no complaints. Everything you did for me is greatly appreciated. You were, and still are, a very important part of my life. Good luck with the windmill, I look forward to some stone ground flour!

Secondly, I would like to thank Dr Karen Walker-Bone. You came to me at just the right time. You are not just a consultant but a truly remarkable, caring and compassionate soul. The NHS needs more like you. You are the best and I love you and see you as one of Earth's Angels. Wherever you are, do not change. You really are an angel and the best doctor any patient could ask for. You are simply the best and I thank you from the bottom of my heart for everything you did for me.

Alistair Rattray is another person I want to thank. You were an angel that appeared, giving me not only great Bowen treatments but also counselling, friendship and humour to Andrew and I at the most dark and difficult times. Thank you.

Mike and Sylvia Golding, thank you for always being there. I could not have asked for better fairy godparents.

Thank you to Burgs. You taught me not only meditation but forgiveness and so much more. You are a shining light, bringing what is needed in these frenetic, somewhat mad times we are living in. I am so grateful for your teachings. Thank you.

Obviously I want to thank every one of my friends who were around (some mentioned in this book and some not). Where would we be without friends?

My biggest thanks go to the many people that visited me, Karen James, Lorraine Butler, Anne Baker, Darcey and Shae Dewse, Laura and Andy Millen, Maddy Booth, Jane Pritchett and Lucy Hendy, Annie Kortenray, John Stone, Jessie Matthews, Mandy Godden, Ken Hamilton and many more. My apologies for anyone not mentioned. You all played enormous roles in keeping me going and staying positive. Thank you.

Thanks also go to Liehsja Blaxland de Lange for your friendship and for coming each week to play your harp and of course, playing on our wedding day. You really are an angel, thank you.

Thank you to Chris Forward for taking me shopping and building my confidence.

Thank you to Bronnie Ware for letting me offload in letters and being my constant friend.

Thank you to Yvonne Loughrey for your friendship, sharing your beautiful children with me and for the Greek Mountain tea that has sustained me through the writing of this book.

Thank you to all the lovely people in my life then and all the special people that have appeared in my life since. Lin Brown you are one of these people. I love your Way Of Creativity retreats and your calm gentle ways and great sense of humour. A great mixture of qualities. Another one of these people is Maggie Smith (and Sarah Phillips) thank you for finding my birth family and the support you have given to me and the adoption community. You are stars. Thank you too to my lunch buddies "the ladies who lunch": Karen James, Anne Baker, Cynthia New and Annie Kortenray. Food and friendship, you can't beat it!!!

The last, but not least, thank you goes to my loving husband, Max Barnes. My life with you is wonderful, thank you for being you, for your love and making me laugh every day. You are the best husband and my best friend and I just adore being with you and sharing my life with you.

Thank you for encouraging and supporting me in the writing of this book. Thank you for providing the photo on the front and back covers and working out the manuscript and actually making it happen. Together we can do anything!

I love you, Spike and River so much xxx

You are all very special and I love you all very much.

9 783732 391851